Delivering Superior Service

Service

Reshaping the Communications
Service Enterprise

René J. Aerdts, Ph.D.
Andreas G. Bauer
Max R. Speur

Bloomington, IN Milton Keynes, UK
authorHOUSE®

AuthorHouse™
1663 Liberty Drive, Suite 200
Bloomington, IN 47403
www.authorhouse.com
Phone: 1-800-839-8640

AuthorHouse™ UK Ltd.
500 Avebury Boulevard
Central Milton Keynes, MK9 2BE
www.authorhouse.co.uk
Phone: 08001974150

First published by AuthorHouse 11/15/2006

ISBN: 978-1-4259-7415-2 (sc)
ISBN: 978-1-4259-7416-9 (hc)

Library of Congress Control Number: 2006909648

Printed in the United States of America
Bloomington, Indiana

This book is printed on acid-free paper.

Table Of Contents

Foreword

The Business Transformation Imperative

"Business transformation is an immediate imperative. For the past few years, most companies have focused on becoming more efficient in an effort to cut costs and reduce operating expenses. That's good—but it's not enough. Service providers must remake their business model. It's innovate or die."

JIM WARNER

VICE CHAIRMAN, TELEMANAGEMENT FORUM

WE ALL LIVE IN world full of challenges. We have challenges in our personal lives. We have challenges at work. Sometimes we are successful in navigating through those challenges, and other times we continue to struggle.

In the dynamic telecommunications industry, we see enterprises struggle with challenges on a day-to-day basis. As some try to respond to the challenges, they still find it difficult to meet customer demand in an efficient and cost-effective way.

Some of the difficulties that we have seen Communications Service Providers (CSPs) try to overcome are:

- *How to create a superior customer experience as a way to differentiate* – Services have changed significantly. Communication service providers provide more than plain old telephone service today.

Consumers demand much more from their providers, so CSPs have to deliver a superior customer experience. To do that, a CSP needs to have an agile operation that can adapt to the rapidly changing needs of consumers today and tomorrow.

- *How to develop, deliver and support next-generation services* – A strong communications company can become a great one if it could deliver a superior customer experience with edge-device products and services. Meeting this consumer demand seamlessly then becomes new revenue sources that substitute traditional voice revenues.

- *How to transform its operations to achieve efficiencies* – The Information Technology (IT) environment for CSPs is highly complex and somewhat limiting to delivering efficient services on a global scale. A CSP has to deliver multiple services to multiple segments, and it has to do it quickly, efficiently and cost effectively. The service provider has to find a way to simplify its operations dramatically so that it can deliver services at the lowest possible cost and remain competitive.

- *How to achieve synergies and economies of scale in post-merger integrations* – In the United States, the industry has continued to consolidate through mergers and acquisitions. In the rest of the world, incumbents are expanding their geographical footprint by acquiring CSPs outside their homelands, thus forming multinational enterprises. Reaping the benefits from synergies and economies of scale is still an open task.

THESE CHALLENGES WILL HAVE a dramatic impact on the business of CSPs in the years ahead. The way a CSP responds to these challenges is crucial to its ultimate success.

As Jim Warner stated, providers have to remake their business model. Delivering services quickly and reducing operating costs requires an IT and operational makeover. EDS believes a transformational change of this kind is imperative to survive in this industry.

EDS wrote a series of industry-specific view-point papers that tackle the major industry issues I described. We combined them into this book to shed light on the complexity of the CSP environment and to provide CSPs with a view on how best to deal with these complex issues.

The following chapter guides you through the book's structure and lays out a series of innovative business transformation initiatives. We intend for this book to give a CSP the necessary steps toward transforming its enterprises to not only survive but also to thrive in an evolving market.

SUE CHEVINS
VICE PRESIDENT
EDS GLOBAL COMMUNICATIONS INDUSTRY

Acknowledgments

WE HOLD DIFFERENT PROFESSIONAL roles. We are business consultants, sales executives and technology architects with different business and technical perspectives. We are a diverse group of leaders drawing from our experiences with clients across all continents.

We are also champions for the communications industry. We wrote viewpoint papers and white papers specifically for the telecom industry. We published an article titled, "Transforming for Customer Loyalty and Growth." The article ran in the TeleManagement Forum's publication, *Telecoms Management: Transformation in 2006.* Publishing that article inspired us to publish a book so that we could give the public a broader and deeper view of the points we made in the article. We decided to publish a compilation of our thought-leadership work that addresses serious challenges for the industry. Our goal is to offer insight on how service providers can gain a competitive edge by undergoing a business and technical transformation.

We thank you for going on the journey with us. As you consider strategies to improve the way you deliver services, we hope you find that this book is a beneficial tool to help you reshape your business so that you can deliver a superior experience to your customers.

Special thanks to our contributors, who spent many hours gathering, writing and refining content. Their vast experience is demonstrated by the compelling knowledge they share in this book.

Special thanks to Eileen Weidman for her efforts in project management, editing and marketing support. And a special thank you to Jon Kemp for his professional writing and editing talent that helped us capture our thoughts on paper.

Thanks also to our senior review team, Sue Chevins, Dennis Stolkey and Lou Keyes for reviewing the final manuscript and providing valuable insight and guidance.

Lastly, thanks to our publisher, AuthorHouse, for bringing our vision to life.

A Note About What To Expect

THIS BOOK PROVIDES THE reader with our point of view on how Communications Service Providers (CSPs) should transform to achieve a series of objectives, from sustaining cost containment to improving the customer experience and loyalty to igniting top-line growth.

The book explains the foundation needed to enable a successful transformation, describes initiatives to create a superior customer experience and discusses our view on how to turn that experience into sustained customer loyalty and revenue growth. Each paper is self-contained to give readers the choice to focus on their particular areas interest.

We have organized the book into four parts, each of which looks at this transformation from a different angle. Each part contains a collection of thought-leadership papers that express our views on current topics.

Part I

PART I IS ABOUT the foundational initiatives needed to enable a successful transformation. We frequently find that CSPs are bogged down by a myriad of inhibitors to transformation, many of which have been created over decades—the so-called legacy environment that tends to create barriers to change and puts the CSP at a cost disadvantage. Part I is about the initiatives a CSP needs to implement in order to transform its legacy environment systematically. We look beyond the low-hanging fruit and envision a program designed to improve the cost economics in a sustainable way and to lay the foundation for a successful business transformation. Business transformation may come in various forms and may affect different aspects of the legacy environment. The papers in Part I cover some of them.

We begin Part I with an introductory paper, "Transformation in Telecommunications," by Max Speur. Using experience from EDS client engagements, Speur outlines the overall transformation approach, how to overcome challenges through transformation and the benefits of transformation.

The paper on "Reducing Complexity Through Application Rationalization" by René Aerdts, explains how a CSP can use industry process-based models to improve the Information Technology (IT) economics in a systematic way through rationalizing the application and underlying IT infrastructure footprint.

The paper on "Agility by Design," co-authored by René Aerdts, Andreas Bauer and Jürgen Donnerstag, describes how to design an agile application architecture by applying a set of principles that allows CSPs to drive both leverage and speed simultaneously.

"Shared Services Center in Telecommunications" paper, authored by Harvey Stotland, extends our transformation theme to enterprise management processes. It offers an overview on how the quality, economics and alignment to the business strategy of administrative enterprise management processes can be improved through a transition into a multi-layered Shared Services Center model.

While the focus, so far, has been on transforming the applications environment, the final two papers of Part I are dedicated to the IT infrastructure. In his paper on "The Data Center of the Future," René Aerdts describes the transformation from a Traditional Data Center model to a Services Data Center model, with special consideration of the business impact of that transition.

The final paper on "The Workplace of the Future," by Andreas Bauer and Harvey Stotland, describes how CSPs can create a superior, cost-efficient workplace environment through the application of automation, mobility and personalization. This paper also discusses how CSPs can apply these same concepts to manage customers' devices, such as Personal Computers (PCs), Personal Digital Assistants (PDAs) and mobile phones. This is an area that many CSPs have identified as a way to expand the services portfolio and to create a superior customer experience.

This discussion directly links into to the next part of the book, which focuses on the end- user experience as a way to create differentiation.

Part II

THE PAPERS IN PART II are about creating points of differentiation in an industry characterized by increasingly commoditized products. In our view, which is shared by many CSPs, creating a superior customer experience is key to differentiation.

The paper on "The Contact Center of the Future in Telecommunications," co-authored by Alberto Balestrazzi, Andreas Bauer and Harvey Stotland, examines how CSPs can achieve a world-class customer experience across all customer touch points while containing cost in a measurable and sustainable way.

The customer experience is also key to success for new service offerings. Internet Protocol Television (IPTV) is a case in point, as it is being perceived by many CSPs as a "killer application" to drive broadband revenues. We believe that only a superior customer experience will entice end users to switch from their current TV providers and become loyal CSP IPTV customers. The paper on "Operationalizing the IPTV Environment," co-authored by Vinod Krishnan, Harvey Stotland and Tara Whitehead, shows exactly how to create such an experience.

Part III

PART III IS ABOUT transforming for loyalty and growth. Certainly, a poor customer experience will often cause a customer to switch to a competitor. But in our view, a superior customer experience alone is not sufficient to retain customers. Today's consumers are all too often attracted by lower price points on similar services or by heavy subsidies on the latest handsets. In our opinion, it takes more than just subsidies, price cuts or loyalty programs to create sustained growth and customer loyalty. CSPs need an ecosystem of partners who jointly create a superior and attractive customer value proposition, building on the unique strengths of each partner. In addition, the underlying enabling technology needs to be put in place as well.

We illustrate our position by opening Part III with a paper on "Revenue Generation for ICT Companies," co-authored by Andreas Bauer and Timothy Samler. This is about convergence in Information and Communications Technology (ICT). CSPs are making significant investments in broadband infrastructures to support data services as a way to re-ignite revenue growth. The key question, however, is how do CSPs turn these investments into continued revenue streams? In other words, how does a CSP monetize data services? The paper discusses our view that a service delivery platform is a necessary, but not a sufficient means to than end. To ensure revenue success, we propose a holistic approach to end-user services and partner programs.

Revenue generation also affects other communications-related businesses. Right now, for examples, CSPs are debating the future of directory services. Some CSPs have decided to divest that business, whereas others see it as an area of significant growth potential. We see Google's success in capturing an important share of the overall advertising market share. Max Speur's paper on "The Future Vision of Directory Services" discusses how technology is driving a revolution in the local advertising business by changing the way customers find, buy and sell online.

Our paper on "A Collaborative ICT Approach," by Alberto Balestrazzi, Andreas Bauer and Paul Morrison shows how product road maps, sales channels and delivery capabilities can be aligned to create a successful partner ecosystem for the ICT marketplace.

A core element in this partnering approach is the collaboration between CSPs and IT service providers. Sebastião Burin's and Renato Osato's paper on "New Models of Collaboration in the ICT Market," discusses the various models now being adopted or considered, and the advantages and drawbacks of each.

Part IV

WE ARE CONVINCED THAT a concerted program of initiatives such as those described in this book will substantially improve the CSP's market position in the medium term. But how can that position be preserved in the long term? We have dedicated Part IV to our view on customer "wants" and "needs" in an increasingly digital world. René Aerdts discusses the impacts of the digital lifestyle on CSPs in "The Agile Telecommunications Customer" paper.

Lastly, we wrap everything up in our "Conclusion and Outlook" section. We reiterate our purpose and intent. We offer an opinion on how CSPs can leverage technology to capture future business opportunities, and we cover future trends in the industry.

We hope you will find it inspiring, helpful and thought provoking. Enjoy reading!

ANDREAS G. BAUER
GLOBAL LEADER
EDS COMMUNICATIONS INDUSTRY FRAMEWORKS

Part I:

Enable a Successful Business Transformation

WE BELIEVE THAT TRANSFORMATION of the IT environment and improvement of cost economics are the first stages a CSP needs to enter and commit to in order to create business value. This section contains view points on initiatives a CSP needs to take to transform to an agile enterprise.

Transformation in Telecommunications

**Evolving the Communications Service
Provider Into an Agile Enterprise**

Max R. Speur

Executive Overview

Convergence has come to the communications marketplace.
Convergence and mobility are now driving the demand for accessible
and affordable products at the network edge. In response to that
shift, a Communications Service Provider (CSP) must move quickly
to evolve its operations, technologies and basic business models.
Forward-looking CSPs are now pursuing this vital transformation.
By adopting a logical, allied approach to this evolution, telecom
organizations can reap its considerable benefits.

This required transformation will be complex, risky and capital-
intensive because most CSPs now rely on highly fragmented
infrastructures that reside on heterogeneous platforms spread
across multiple networks.

3

The author describes challenges the communications industry faces and how to overcome those challenges through transformation. He also outlines the benefits of undergoing a business and technical transformation.

Reshaping the CSP

CONVERGENCE IS A REALITY in today's communications landscape. As a result, a CSP is expected to offer products and services that are integrated seamlessly across its networks and to deliver a unique, high-quality customer experience more quickly than ever before.

This convergence has produced a proliferation of devices at the network edge. Consumers expect those devices to use a single connection, to be customized to their specific work and lifestyle needs and to be delivered at an attractive price point.

CSPs recognize and understand these trends but face key challenges in transforming to take full advantage of these opportunities in an increasingly competitive environment. Today's communications landscape is defined by the following:

- **Rapid Decline of Traditional Public Switched Telephone Network (PSTN)-Based Revenues** – This trend has been driven by deregulation and the displacement of old business systems by new Internet-oriented technologies.
- **Slow Uptake of Data Services** – While the manufacturers of televisions, audio gear and other consumer electronics have talked for years about blending products with personal computers— and giving consumers an "anywhere/anytime" stream of data, video and music—it has not happened. The industries do not as yet have compatible technology standards, and high-speed Internet connections have not been widespread enough to drive the emergence of data services.
- **Increased Willingness of Consumers to Churn** – Subscribers often say they leave a provider because communications products

and services are complex, poorly integrated, not personalized and too expensive.

TECHNOLOGICAL CONVERGENCE IS POSSIBLE, and it is happening. But the true challenge for today's CSP is the need to connect this new generation of edge devices in a way that delivers a seamless, personalized, easy-to-use and affordable communications experience to the consumer. That is why forward-looking CSPs are now planning and pursuing a fundamental transformation.

Adopting the Factory Model

TO ENSURE A QUALITY consumer experience, CSPs must adopt an integrated "factory" approach to the management and delivery of data-oriented products and services. This factory-based vision is characterized by the following:

- It provides a platform for the delivery of truly integrated applications and services. In most instances, this will require the upgrading and integration of the CSP's networks.
- It offers a consistent customer experience across multiple devices and networks.
- It typically requires the streamlining and simplification of order-to-cash processes.
- It operates at a low fixed-cost base and can scale cost-effectively as volumes grow faster than revenues.
- It is aligned with the needs of the consumer and provides a seamless customer experience through close linkages with channel management.

TODAY, FEW CSPS HAVE the capabilities of this factory-based model. Most CSPs use system environments and infrastructures that are highly fragmented, with legacy applications residing on heterogeneous platforms layered cross multiple networks.

These fragmented infrastructures—including applications, databases, interfaces and other IT elements—are costly and difficult to operate. They do not allow more effective service delivery, and they do not serve the data-oriented segments of the market well.

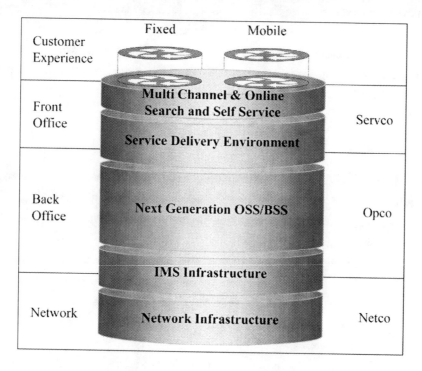

Figure 1 – The CSP's Future Converged Business Architecture

The CSP's objective is to provide converged services, allowing end users to access video, data and voice services seamlessly, regardless of their living or working environments.

The Agile Enterprise: A Vision for Transforming the CSP

TRANSFORMATION IS A HOT topic in the telecommunications industry because of the major changes now sweeping the sector. Those changes include shifts in financing, regulation, systems, processes and customer expectations.

A Paradigm Shift

A CSP MUST ADAPT its strategic intent and supporting core competences to meet changing customer demands and technology requirements. The industry can now create new business models built on a completely new paradigm and driven by creative new competences. Examples of companies adopting these new models include Yahoo! and Google, "pure players" that now offer free voice services in addition to their traditional services and are rapidly becoming online merchants.

These new offerings are typically built on unique new business models. Google's primary source of income, for example, is Internet advertising, while most CSP revenue streams come from charging consumers per bundle for the use of a particular infrastructure-based service.

To compete and succeed in the emerging converged environment, a CSP must begin a multi-year business transformation that will result in the innovation of its core competences. This change process will involve several waves over a period of time. Attempts to shortcut this change process often lead to dead ends and higher costs and seldom produce a satisfying result.

The Agile CSP

AS DEMONSTRATED IN FIGURE 1, the future vision for an agile CSP incorporates three distinct entities:

- **Netco** – The Network Company
- **Opco** – The Operation Company
- **Servco** – The Service Company

These can exist as independent companies or as integrated business units leveraging each other's assets. Each of these entities has unique business models, much like the oil industry, where "upstream" and "downstream" operating units complement and reinforce one another.

These business units must operate separately because they require very different core competences. A netco, for example, must strive to create operational excellence. An opco must create product excellence. A servco seeks customer intimacy. Those unique core competences determine the ability of each entity to compete and succeed over the long term in a specific market.

Unfortunately, few CSPs now have this practical, competence-driven structure. When we examine the majority of CSPs around the world, virtually all have built a complicated plethora of processes, legacy systems and modern systems to support a single business model and core competence: the operation and maintenance of a PSTN network. But in today's converged environment, that PSTN-based model is no longer adequate, as associated revenues and margins are shrinking rapidly.

The imperatives for CSPs are clear. They must pursue top-line growth through investments in next-generation platforms. They must reduce cost and complexity by bringing the benefits of agility, such as speed and leverage, to their organizations. And they must reallocate current operating expenditure (opex) and capital expenditure (capex) toward initiatives to deliver higher business value to their organizations.

According to META Group, 80 percent of a CSP's annual opex goes to running, maintaining and upgrading their current complicated environments. Seventeen percent goes to enhancing the current environment, and only three percent is directed toward strategically investing in new core competencies.

By redirecting investments and modernizing the legacy and current environment, CSPs can reduce cost and complexity. The resulting savings can free up capital for investments in the strategic platforms needed to support new core competences. A CSP can thus equip itself to deliver integrated applications and services and can invest in the infrastructure needed to meet the demands of future traffic volumes cost effectively, as noted in Figure 2.

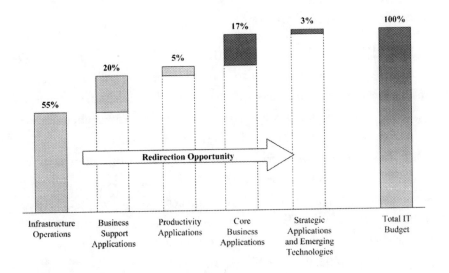

Figure 2 – Redirection Opportunity (Illustrative)

Source: Meta Group Worldwide IT Trends and Benchmark Report

A CSP can leverage this reinvestment process to transform its businesses in a way that is proven, incremental and potentially self-funding. Delivering on this vision will dramatically change the CSP experience at each level of operation.

At the netco level, the CSP will gain:

- A common, integrated experience across networks and devices

At the opco level, the CSP will experience:

- Fast, first-time resolution of queries and requests
- Fewer faults, often resolved before the customer is affected
- High level of automation

At the servco level, the CSP can deliver:

- Self-service when needed
- Instant activation
- One-touch, one-click, one-request performance
- Measurably improved subscriber service and satisfaction

A Transformation Pathway

TO ACHIEVE THOSE CAPABILITIES, CSPs must build an agile enterprise platform capable of meeting the core business architectural and operational requirements of the netco, opco and servco entities. Building such a platform is a journey, and calls for a comprehensive road map to guide the CSP in its evolution toward agility.

EDS recommends a transformational framework known as the BATOG: **B**usiness Context, **A**pplication Portfolio, **T**echnology Infrastructure, **O**rganizational Capability, **G**overnance Model. BATOG can be used to document a CSP's current reality and future vision, to identify the gap between the two, and to create the plans and road map needed to achieve that objective (see Figure 3).

	Current Reality	THE GAP	Future Vision
(B)	**Business Context**	• Optimize capex and opex • Improve customer experience • Reduce churn • Accelerate speed to market	**Business Context**
(A)	**Application Portfolio**	• Massively reduce duplication and complexity • Build a leveraged architecture across services • Seamlessly integrate application and content providers	**Application Portfolio**
(T)	**Technology Infrastructure**	• Minimize the risk of migration to IP networks • Blend IT and network technology • Achieve interoperability • Standardize to achieve economies of scale	**Technology Infrastructure**
(O)	**Organizational Capability**	• Manage innovation • Manage blurring boundaries between network and IT • Transition to "one factory" model	**Organizational Capability**
(G)	**Governance**	• Manage the transformation effectively • Re-skill existing resources • Balance investments in new vs. maintaining existing technologies	**Governance**

Figure 3: Transformational Framework

Business Context

TO ENSURE A SUCCESSFUL transformation, a CSP should adopt a long-term strategic view of its business and business agenda and then take an incremental approach to implementing the transformation plan. This puts a strong focus on delivering business value at every milestone. A transformation plan should be based on the CSP's business agenda and should leverage industry best practices and capabilities.

Application Portfolio and Technology Infrastructure

CSPS MUST ALSO UNDERSTAND where they are, where they want to go and how they will get there. They must examine how many outdated, inflexible business systems they have and how they can modernize them to support new services and business models. Industry standards-based frameworks are available from the TeleManagement Forum, for example the enhanced Telecom Operations Map® (eTOM), to analyze current CSP situations, evaluate network proliferation and create a vision for a future service-oriented architecture. This architecture will enable end-to-end service capabilities, agility and the ability to manage the demand at the network edge, thus dramatically improving the customer experience.

Organizational Capability and Governance Model

ORGANIZATIONAL CAPABILITIES AND GOVERNANCE are essential elements of any transformation plan. CSPs must ensure they have the organizational capabilities—either internally or from external partners—to deliver the products and service quality customers expect. Governance defines how the components of the operational model work together and harmonize IT across the enterprise to form a functioning whole and to show they will improve top-line growth.

Transformation Execution

EXECUTION OF THE TRANSFORMATION happens in parallel streams. Stream 1 consists of rolling out the new systems. Stream 2 addresses the modernization and/or decommissioning of legacy and existing systems.

To ensure the integrity of the transformation vision, the legacy environment should be carefully assessed early in the transformation program. The goal of this evolution is to identify in advance the systems and structures that need to change and to remove any obstacles to change.

Our analysis reveals that in the initial stage of the transformation program, legacy modernization generates significant short-term benefits.

The savings and efficiencies achieved in this early stage also prepare the CSP for the longer-term transformational journey. Once the newer systems cut over into production, additionally gained efficiencies can be used to accelerate the transformation.

Examples of transformational initiatives to achieve efficiencies include the following:

- Decommissioning or redesigning of the business silos which, given the changes in markets and technology, have become obsolete
- Using business frameworks such as eTOM to convert the business to a future-state architecture and align the processes to that structure
- Modernizing outdated fulfillment, assurance and billing systems
- Redesigning and integrating service delivery environments and go-to-market models
- Introducing the integrated products and services needed to build a sustainable competitive advantage
- Redesigning and modernizing the enterprise integration layer, ensuring organization-wide data integrity

This approach, executed on average in three-to-five years, will enable enterprise agility. Working with selected partners, this approach gives CSPs new core competences and end-to-end service management capabilities. This alliance-based strategy achieves a true business ecosystem where company boundaries completely blur, and more importantly, where the "factory" environment is scalable to manage the increase in volumes created by the demand at the edge.

Benefits of the Transformation

THE BENEFIT OF ANY business transformation lies in the outcomes that the collaborating parties provide to each other.

From a financial perspective, the CSP seeks to optimize opex and capex across the business, generate new revenue streams through new core competences and redirect savings to strategic investments that yield maximum return.

Looking at the benefits from a customer and operational perspective, CSPs seek to accelerate time-to-market for new products and services. CSPs also want to improve the customer experience through faster call handling, service activation and order completion times; fewer inquiries-per-bill; more orders completed online; and an increase in the number of faults resolved on the first call.

By improving customer satisfaction, service availability and capacity utilization, CSPs can improve customer loyalty and reduce churn.

From a people, system and technology perspective, CSPs can also minimize the migration risk through transformation governance, achieve leverage and simplicity throughout the organization, and control headcounts and cost-per-call.

Conclusion

THE FORCES OF MOBILITY and convergence are rapidly changing the communications marketplace. CSPs now face a market in which traditional sources of revenue are declining, new competitors are emerging, and subscribers expect new and higher levels of communications service.

To survive and succeed in that environment, CSPs must move quickly to revise and modernize internal operations, IT infrastructures and fundamental business strategies. Astute CSPs can pursue this important evolution by leveraging the methods and resources of a proven transformation model.

Our vision for CSP transformation suggests an agile, factory-oriented future state that addresses all network, operational and service requirements. We advocate a proven, business-driven methodology that hundreds of companies have used to achieve strategic business transformation.

By applying this transformational approach and resources, CSPs can achieve measurable cost savings, improve operational efficiencies, and drive both customer satisfaction and bottom-line results.

Endnotes

Darlin, Damon. *The Australian Financial Review.* "Many Machines, Soon One Connection."

Hamel, Gary and Lisa Valikangas. Harvard Business Review On Point. "The Quest for Resilience," September 1, 2003.

Kaplan, Robert S and David P. Norton. Balanced Scorecard: Translating Strategy into Action.

Kotter, John P. *Leading Change.* 1996.

Kotter, John P. Harvard Business Review On Point. "Why Transformation Efforts Fail," Winter 2005.

Porter, Michael E. Porter. Competitive Advantage: Creating and Sustaining Superior Performance.

About the Author

Max R. Speur has had significant international experience in the communications industry in Europe and Asia Pacific. He is currently the Asia Pacific communications industry leader for EDS. In this role, Speur is responsible for innovation, thought leadership and demand creation, and for enabling clients' growth. Speur was previously with IBM Global Services, where he served as business development executive on a variety of engagements in Thailand, China, India and Australia.

Reducing Complexity Through Application Rationalization

Managing Scope and Complexity Through Industry Process-Based Models

RENÉ J. AERDTS, PH.D.

Executive Overview

Most Communications Service Providers (CSPs) will agree that the top global issues in the industry include speed-to-market, convergence, consolidation and cost reduction. As these items cross the business and Information Technology (IT) realm, an integrated approach toward providing solutions in support of these issues is necessary.

One of these approaches is application rationalization, where the applications in support of the business function are analyzed and rationalized. This rationalization takes the form of elimination of functions and applications and consolidation of applications and servers.

The author describes how CSPs can reduce complexity by rationalizing applications and the underlying IT infrastructure footprint. He provides detailed descriptions of the steps involved.

Application Rationalization

THE APPROACH TOWARD APPLICATION rationalization in the communications industry, described in this paper, is to manage the application scope and complexity through industry process-based models. The enhanced Telecom Operations Map® (eTOM) is the standard business process framework used by service providers and suppliers within the industry. The eTOM framework describes the business processes required by a service provider and breaks them down into varying levels of detail according to their significance and priority for the business.

In our experience at EDS, the eTOM model provides a sound framework for segmenting the applications portfolio into bite-sized elements. The eTOM process model is used to aggregate individual applications into meaningful business functions for analyzing and making recommendations. These individual applications are cataloged and costed into the various process and sub-process levels within eTOM for analysis and creating recommendations. In most client environments, the eTOM process model requires customization to meet the specific client business processes and organization structures.

An engagement team is typically organized into tracks, each focused on a high-level business process category defined. Each track includes a telecommunications industry expert and executes the following tasks:

- Develop an application strategy to determine the long-term set of applications to best support the business.
- Prioritize opportunities based on our financial baseline.
- Review work stream opportunities with the client to ensure agreement and build support.
- Develop detailed financial analysis and implementation plan as input to the business case.

MULTIPLE ENGAGEMENTS HAVE SHOWN that maximum savings can be achieved through a combined IT and business process alignment.

Communications Industry

ACCORDING TO AN A.T. Kearney global survey of CEOs, "37% of surveyed executives consider *technology alignment with business strategy and integrating existing technology* to be the strategic issue of most concern."[1] Based on the rapidly changing nature of regulatory requirements, consolidation, technology advancement, and technology roll out in the communications industry, it is not surprising that alignment of technology with the business needs—especially from an application perspective—is a strategic concern.

Typically, storage and server consolidation provide potential quick-hit opportunities for many clients. Application rationalization, on the other hand, is required to drive beyond the low hanging fruit for maximum benefits, including operational, engineering, and utilities strategies:

- Operational Strategies – Include reduction of operational cost in the form of rationalization, centralization, consolidation, leverage of skills and technology deployment.
- Engineering Strategies – Include replacement of technology diversity and complexity with standard, leveraged and integrated solutions.
- Utilities Strategies – Include optimization of resource utilization, delivery time, flexibility, recoverability, leading to a utility computing environment.

---

[1] A.T. Kearney Press Release Quote. "E-Business has CEOs confused, according to A.T. Kearney's global study of 251 CEOs," July 13, 2000.

Top Issues

LIKE ANY INDUSTRY AT the moment, the communications industry is challenged from a financial point of view. Increased competition, cost competitiveness and operational cost containment are just some of the examples that drive businesses to align IT with business. However, in this industry the situation is worsened by the overspending in the mid-to-late 1990s and the rapid drop in telecommunications end-user Average Revenue per User (ARPU), combined with moderate growth. The four major business issues in the industry are speed-to-market, convergence, consolidation and cost reduction. Each one of these areas calls for specific integrated industry solutions, each consisting of one or more solutions components:

- **Speed-to-Market** – In today's competitive market place, being first-to-market is a key market differentiator and competitive advantage. As the competitive advantage gap—the time between the conception of an idea and bringing that idea to market—decreases every year, a company needs to minimize the lag time between these points in time through leverage and speed.

- **Convergence** – According to Webster, convergence refers to coming together and uniting in a common interest or focus. As such, convergence in the communications industry occurs at several levels:

  o Company – The industry continues to go through convergence. As a result, information technologies, product lines and business processes need to be integrated and consolidated, from CSP and end-user perspectives.

  o Products – As new products are rolled out (or are added to the existing suite through acquisitions and mergers), end users request and expect an integrated suite of products and services so that they can make informed buying decisions, and security and privacy is extremely high on this list of expectations. Convergence on voice and data has a dramatic impact on the underlying applications required to support new product offerings to both mass market and enterprise customers. Furthermore, product bundling requires the IT organization to add functionality to support these.

o Technology – The integration of technologies is a never-ending battle, and even though integration and middleware provide solutions in this technology convergence, more companies are moving toward platform, storage, and application consolidation. This move reduces complexity and simplifies the integration of the underlying systems and applications.

- **Consolidation** – As mentioned above, technology consolidation is important. However, equally important is the integration and convergence of the services that provide support for a corporation.
- **Cost Reduction** – With the current focus on financials, cost reduction is a critical component of every information technology project or program. As services are combined, servers and storage consolidated and data flows integrated, the cost savings to be achieved are a critical factor in the decision process to proceed.

The focus of this paper is primarily on cost reduction for the purposes of redirecting these savings into more value-aligned areas within the overall CSP business strategy.

Cost Reductions

ACCORDING TO AN A.T. Kearney study[2], between 75 and 90 percent of IT budgets are allocated to the ongoing operations of the infrastructure. This breakdown implies that only between 10 and 25 percent of the IT budget is available for new opportunities and for creating future business value, including development of new applications.

As IT expenditures on new development and IT budgets are decreasing due to economic issues, many companies plan cuts in head count and consulting services to help meet reduced budget targets. As a result, most IT departments aim to reduce fixed expenses associated with infrastructure and

---

[2] Clare, Gary and Christian Hagen, Jim Shand. AT Kearney Executive Agenda Vol. 6 No. 1. "Maximizing Value from IT Investments," First Quarter 2003.

software license fees in order to reallocate current IT expenses to investments that deliver higher business value.

Inefficiencies in IT

MOST CSPS HAVE A large and diverse installed base of hardware, software and (often proprietary) applications that run all (or part) of critical business functions. It is critical that these investments yield true business benefits to the CSP. As is shown in Figure 1, the more mature an IT organization is, the more business value it will derive from the investments in IT.

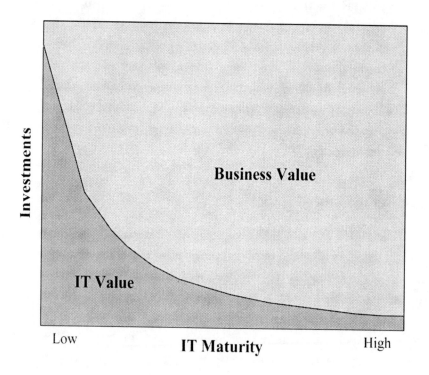

Figure 1 – IT and Business Alignment

As IT organizations mature, business processes tend to drive the IT investments. Given the fact that many of the investments are made to improve the service provider's financials, it is critical that operational inefficiencies get eliminated. Some of the major inefficiencies that drive incremental cost across the industry include the following:

- **Misalignment of IT Activity to Corporate Strategy** – In the past, organizations often introduced new technology without regard to business benefits. In the current business environment, technology deployment is driven by business needs. However, because of legacy applications and rapidly changing business requirements, there is still an ongoing misalignment of IT strategy to the corporate business strategy.

- **Lack of Effective Business or IT Governance** – In almost every business, the IT costs usually form a large component of the overall cost of a corporation. It is critical that these costs are managed and controlled effectively at a corporate level. As such, the existence of a business-level IT governance function— responsible to oversee the allocation of funds for IT and determine the business value derived from these investments—is a critical function that needs to be put in place.

- **Proliferation of Applications** – As the number of applications grows, so does the complexity. This complexity is derived from the interconnectivity of disparate systems as well as the operational aspects related to the management of the systems.

- **Duplication of Functionality, Systems and Support Infrastructure** – As the number of systems and applications increases due to growth or mergers and acquisitions, the number of functions and subsystems that are duplicated increases. This duplication requires additional infrastructure resources like data storage, processing needs and support staff.

- **Operations Performed in Silos** – Even though information technology has evolved since the 1960s, a large portion of information and data processing still occurs in silos. This silo mentality leads to duplication and inefficiencies in processing, which in turn leads to a negative customer experience as a result of incomplete and difficult-to-reconcile information. Enterprises end up having multiple inconsistent sources of truth that defeats the basic purpose of their existence.

- **Inappropriate Enhancement and Use of Systems** – In many organizations, individual departments still have the authority to make changes or enhancements to systems that will carry a company-wide impact, a result of the aforementioned silo mentality that came about in the 1960s and 1970s. At the same time, this type of mentality also leads to an inappropriate use of those systems (as these systems are sub-optimized for departmental use), possibly resulting in a company-wide degradation of the overall IT environment.

- **Fragmented Information Architecture** – In many corporations, an end-to-end enterprise architecture does not exist. Oftentimes, a department-level architecture exists, but no effort is made to tie these individual architectures together into a true enterprise-wide architecture. As a result, the overall information architecture is fragmented at best, and in some instances, the architecture does not exist at all. Buying decisions are made based on the "vendor-of-the-day" selections, resulting in true fragmentation of the architecture, and operational complexities.

As inefficiencies are tied to cost, it is imperative to look at the total IT spend. A typical IT spend breakdown is shown in Figure 2.

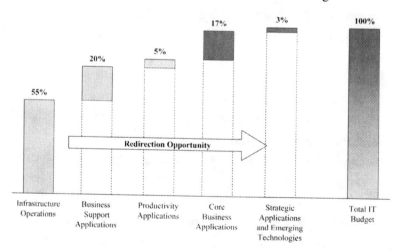

Figure 2 – Typical IT Spend (Illustrative)

Source: Meta Group Worldwide IT Trends and Benchmark Report

Industry statistics indicate that around 80 percent of costs on infrastructure and support personnel are being spent on maintaining ongoing operations, while only 20 percent of IT budgets go toward new opportunities to create future business value. At the same time, IT capital budgets and IT expenditures on new development are decreasing, mainly because of economic issues.

As a result of these inefficiencies, many corporations do not derive the maximum benefit from the investments in infrastructure and information technology components; however, through initiatives like server and storage consolidation and rationalization combined with application rationalization, a CSP will make significant strides toward improving IT efficiency and improved IT and business alignment, resulting in a sustainable improvement of IT economics.

More importantly, inefficiencies can lead to lost market opportunities. A service provider's foresight and responsiveness to external factors, such as value chain restructuring or regulatory changes, determines whether the CSP drives, thrives or simply survives. As these types of changes occur at an increasing pace, it is critical that the underlying information technology environment is flexible and agile enough to rapidly respond to these types of business challenges.

Agile Enterprise

AGILITY IS AN INNOVATIVE way of doing business that involves an organization's ability to anticipate changing market dynamics, adapt to those dynamics and accelerate its changes faster than its competitors to create economic value.

Agility combines flexible business processes, a solid technology foundation and empowered people. With these elements in place, an enterprise can increase its economic value in spite of changing market dynamics—unlike a non-agile enterprise that suffers from fluctuations as the market changes.

An agile enterprise is an enterprise that takes advantage of agility by thriving on market changes. An agile infrastructure provides the foundation, from an IT perspective, to enable an enterprise to combine leverage and speed into agility.

While many businesses focus on optimizing factors such as speed, cost and quality as independent issues, the agile enterprise employs a more holistic approach, emphasizing five levers of agility: visibility, velocity, flexibility, quality and efficiency, each to a targeted degree.

IT Transformation

AS THE PREVIOUS SECTIONS of this paper show, the alignment of IT and business is critical to the survival of businesses, especially the telecommunications industry. Based on the IT challenges outlined previously, it is critical that an IT transformation takes place. This IT transformation takes into account the infrastructure (hardware, software and networks), as well as the applications. The rationalization of these two areas as a single entity provides a CSP with the greatest benefits.

The Overall Approach

IN GENERAL, THE IT transformation approach takes the form of an IT Portfolio Optimization, which consists of a series of rationalization approaches to optimize and improve the economics of IT. These rationalization approaches include an end-to-end view of IT and consist of seven major dimensions (see Figure 3). It is important to notice that the dimensions are interdependent on one another. The primary focus of this paper is on application and infrastructure rationalization and the use of selective IT outsourcing (as indicated by the dotted line in Figure 3.) to improve the economics of IT.

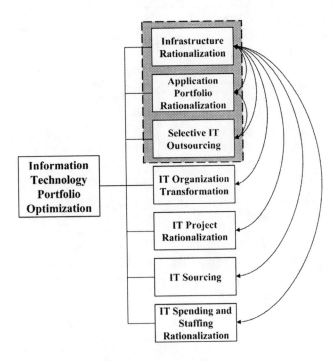

Figure 3 – IT Portfolio Optimization Interdependencies

Figure 3 shows an iterative loop from Applications Portfolio Rationalization back to Infrastructure Rationalization—as additional savings can be found once the Applications Rationalization is complete, maximizing benefits. Some of the major characteristics for each of these functions are described in Table 1.

Function	Description	Areas Addressed
Infrastructure Rationalization	This component is the first in the optimization process, as it focuses on the foundation of the applications: the infrastructure, where a CSP can achieve some of the quick hits.	• Optimize current assets, leveraging capacity across the various business needs. • Quantify the savings that could be achieved by moving to alternate offshore infrastructure support. • Consolidate disparate servers, storage, network and support infrastructures across the enterprise.
Application Portfolio Rationalization	This component has a strong interaction with the Infrastructure Rationalization component and focuses on the application areas.	• Eliminate low value business applications and associated support costs. • Consolidate redundant applications, functionality and support. • Quantify the savings that could be achieved by moving to alternate application support.
Selective IT Outsourcing	As a CSP moves back to its roots and focuses on its core business, outsourcing non-core components of the business is a growing trend. From an IT perspective, both infrastructure and application management are affected.	• Infrastructure – Assess internal IT capabilities and spend against industry benchmarks and alternative service arrangements (including, but not limited to data center, network, workplace and help-desk services). • Applications – Identify legacy or non-core business applications that can be outsourced to allow internal IT resources to be reallocated to higher value efforts. • The key is to identify opportunities that improve service levels, while achieving cost targets.

Table 1 – IT Portfolio Optimization Components

Function	Description	Areas Addressed
IT Organization Transformation	Changing and overhauling an IT infrastructure and environment can only be successful if the supporting organization, processes and procedures change at the same time to show IT changes.	• Establish consistent processes for delivery of new projects and ongoing maintenance activities. • Define governance model, ensuring clearly defined roles and responsibilities. • Identify alternative organizational models that better align to business needs.
IT Project Rationalization	At a more detailed level, all individual projects that support the transformation need to be identified, prioritized, rationalized and staffed.	• Prioritize projects across the enterprise to optimize the IT investment portfolio and maximize returns/benefits. • Rationalize projects to eliminate discretionary or low value initiatives. • Accelerate benefits where possible. • Align with business priorities. • This is an important component of the overall process, as it can be implemented as a continuous process that can be managed by the CSP.
IT Sourcing	The Infrastructure and Application Portfolio Rationalization will result in a different mix of hardware and software needed to support the business. This change implies that these areas need to be addressed:	• Assess external spend on products and services. • Centralize vendor negotiations and management. • Consolidate total enterprise spend to gain negotiating leverage with vendors. • Define complementary IT partnership model.
IT Spending and Staffing Rationalization	As the Infrastructure and Application Portfolio Rationalization yields benefits, it is critical that IT spend and staffing requirements show the updated infrastructure and IT environment.	• Assess IT spending and staffing against appropriate industry benchmarks. • Determine areas to reduce IT-base spending and redirect spending to higher-value areas.

Table 1 – IT Portfolio Optimization Components *continued*

The Methodology

AS MENTIONED EARLIER, THE primary focus of this paper is on Application and Infrastructure Rationalization and the use of selective IT outsourcing to improve the economics of IT. These three areas are the ones within an IT Portfolio Optimization engagement that are addressed first.

The remainder of the paper focuses on the first two activities: Application Portfolio Rationalization and Infrastructure Rationalization. The recommended methodology takes a phased approach, with key deliverables and implementations at specific points in time to reap value as soon as possible.

Approach to Application and Infrastructure Rationalization

THE APPROACH TO APPLICATION Portfolio Infrastructure Rationalization focuses on delivering value through a series of implementation waves, by providing specific business benefits approximately every three-to-six months. The purpose of this waved implementation approach is to use the early savings to invest in more capital intense areas needing improvement. Application Portfolio and Infrastructure Rationalization follows a four-phased approach:

- **Phase I – The Pre-Rationalization Diagnostic Phase** focuses on identifying high-level business goals, collecting data on infrastructure and applications. scoping out the opportunities, and building a business case for rationalization.
- **Phase II – The Rationalization Design Phase** focuses on the creation of the "to-be" state and a transformation plan. This phase considers simultaneously both infrastructure and applications for which detailed rationalization road maps are developed.
- **Phase III – The Application Rationalization Phase** is and execution and focuses on specific categories of applications, in order to drive down portfolio complexity by consolidating functionality, retiring and/or redesigning applications to better align with stated business objective at optimal cost. This phase

also provides a natural bridge into infrastructure rationalization by embarking on the server decommissioning process.

- **Phase IV – The Infrastructure Rationalization Phase** is and execution focuses on reducing operations costs by consolidating and pooling hardware resources across data centers, facilities, business units, geographies and product lines.

It is important to notice that during Phase II, two simultaneous paths are pursued: the infrastructure and application planning. As these two phases are closely intertwined, considerable interaction between these planning phases occurs, resulting in the capability to have Phase III and Phase IV run more or less concurrently. As the Application Portfolio Rationalization usually requires more preparation work, the Application Rationalization Phase is usually initiated slightly earlier than the Infrastructure Rationalization Phase[3].

A diagnostic study should be considered as a "front-end" project to a full IT transformation program that explicitly ties to business value accumulation. This is key to success in a multi-year change program (see Figure 4).

---

[3] As applications depend on the underlying infrastructure component, application assessment can be viewed as the first step in this process.

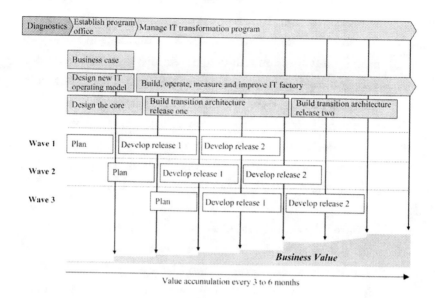

Figure 4 – Application and Infrastructure
Rationalization Engagement (Illustrative)

In many cases, a specific program is required to complete the identified activities because of the scope and impact to the overall business. Many CSPs choose to initiate an IT transformation program, which guides the CSP through the technology and business changes required for the successful implementation and sustained support for a major project or program that crosses organizational boundaries.

Application Portfolio Diagnostic Study

BEFORE A COMPLETE IT Portfolio Optimization can occur, a complete portfolio view needs to be created that can then be optimized and rationalized. A typical three-month diagnostics study consists of four steps.

1. Review IT vision, objectives and strategy; define scope of rationalization.
2. Collect data on current state ("as-is") and identify rationalization opportunities.

3. Assess current state and develop rationalization approach; perform high level cost/benefit analysis.
4. Build business case; define transformation strategy and high level implementation plan.

The diagnostic study is critical to defining the exact scope and articulating a clear path toward IT Portfolio Optimization.

Application Rationalization Options

SEVERAL OPTIONS TO RATIONALIZE applications may be considered, including the following:

1. **Applications Consolidation** – Identifies, evaluates, and consolidates applications that have similar business functionality to create a common set across the portfolio.
2. **Applications Co-Existence** – Identifies which applications can reside together on the same server to allow physical consolidation of servers.
3. **Applications Reengineering** – Identifies legacy applications for extension (i.e., enhancements) or renewal to better meet the requirements of the business environment.
4. **Applications Decommissioning** – Identifies applications that have limited business value and high operational cost that can be eliminated.

Each option is considered during the four-step diagnostics approach described above. Each step takes into account the business and technology value, as well as the risk and cost.

Transformation and Business Process Alignment

AFTER IDENTIFYING THE DEGREE of strategy alignment (see Figure 6), these applications are mapped to business processes using the customized process taxonomy (see Figure 5). Next, an assessment of the technical and functional quality from the business perspective is performed, with specific values assigned to each intersection of application and business function.

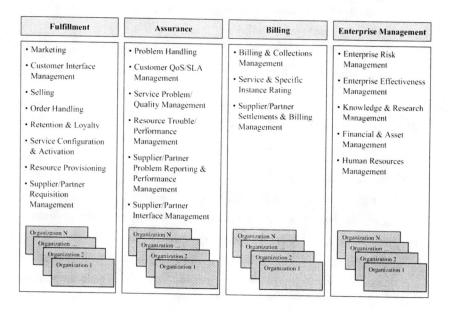

Fulfillment	Assurance	Billing	Enterprise Management
• Marketing	• Problem Handling	• Billing & Collections Management	• Enterprise Risk Management
• Customer Interface Management	• Customer QoS/SLA Management	• Service & Specific Instance Rating	• Enterprise Effectiveness Management
• Selling	• Service Problem/ Quality Management	• Supplier/Partner Settlements & Billing Management	• Knowledge & Research Management
• Order Handling	• Resource Trouble/ Performance Management		• Financial & Asset Management
• Retention & Loyalty			
• Service Configuration & Activation	• Supplier/Partner Problem Reporting & Performance Management		• Human Resources Management
• Resource Provisioning			
• Supplier/Partner Requisition Management	• Supplier/Partner Interface Management		

Figure 5 – eTOM-Based Process Model Approach

The eTOM process model is used to guide a seven-step approach: catalog, manage, strategize, prioritize, review, analyze and link.

1. **Catalog** – This step focuses on individual applications that are cataloged and costed into levels within the eTOM process model for analysis and creating recommendations.

2. **Manage** – This step focuses on the collection and alignment of resources, industry, process and cross-functional experts. These resources are managed through a project and program management structure. It is critical that executive oversight is in place and that project managers and advisors, as well as subject matter experts, are available. The cross-functional teams consist of an architecture and project support team.

3. **Strategize** – An application strategy is being developed to determine the long-term set of applications to best support the business. Each of the applications is categorized into one of four

categories—single suite, strategic, legacy and niche—based on the degree of business value and business reach (see Figure 6).

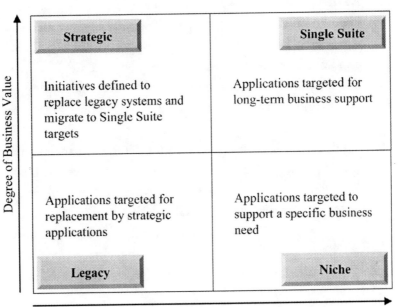

Figure 6 – Application Portfolio Strategy Matrix

4. **Prioritize** – Next, each of the identified opportunities is prioritized based on the financial baseline. By using a cost filter against the identified opportunities from the catalog step, each of the opportunities is categorized and prioritized into one of the following two areas:

   - Do Not Consider – This category consists of all those applications that are removed from considerations because of cost, technical or business issues (such as corporate initiatives).

   - Consider – This category consists of all those applications that are candidates for rationalization, including consolidation, reengineering, decommissioning and lower-cost alternatives. Each one of these categories of candidates is prioritized based on the business value, technical value, risk, and cost.

5. **Review** – The next step consists of a review of the work-stream opportunities with the company to build support and ensure agreement. The six sub-steps include: opportunity identification, opportunity validation (followed by "go" or "no go" decision), financial and technical analysis, solution development approach, opportunity profile development and opportunity profile review.

6. **Analyze** – For each opportunity, a detailed financial analysis and implementation plan is developed as input to the business case. The business case focuses on two major components:

    • Opportunity Financials – The opportunity financial addresses cost reconciliation, Full-Time Equivalent (FTE) staffing requirements, implementation cost, and benefits and savings by time line, resulting in the business case.

    • Opportunity Profile – The opportunity profile includes the opportunity summary, business and technical assessment, qualitative benefits, net cost and savings and implementation time line.

7. **Link** – Finally, the process closely links the IT and business transformation program to provide greater cost reduction returns. It is important to have a single entity (either internal or external) that is accountable for both the IT and business effort in order to streamline decision-making, to improve the communications, and to minimize the overall project costs. A sample cost savings scenario is shown in Figure 7.

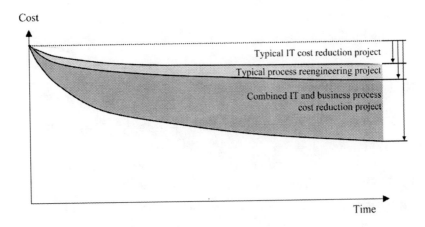

Figure 7 – Sample Cost Savings Scenario (Illustrative)

Conclusion

THE TELECOMMUNICATIONS INDUSTRY IS going through dynamic changes. The market for voice services is saturated, but revenue from data services is picking up slowly, leading to a flat ARPU. However, CSPs are making significant investments in Next Generation Networks (NGN), which need to be recouped in the medium and long term. Under these circumstances, a CSP need to focus strategically on achieving sustainable cost reduction by reducing its non-discretionary spending and redirecting savings into areas that support expanding new business revenue opportunities.

Application Portfolio and Infrastructure Rationalization is a solution to excessive applications and server proliferation, ineffective application portfolios and costly applications maintenance. It consists of a set of proven methods that deliver value by rationalizing the service provider's applications and infrastructure into a more efficient portfolio, addressing key issues like proliferation of applications, duplication of functionalities, excessive systems interfacing or siloed application architectures—all of which lead to high maintenance costs.

Information Technology Portfolio Optimization provides a systematic approach to reduce IT costs in a sustainable way while extracting higher business value from IT.

About the Author

René J. Aerdts, Ph.D., is an EDS fellow. He is part of the Information Technology Outsourcing (ITO) Service Delivery organization, which is responsible for the IT component service delivery. The title of EDS fellow is awarded to the corporation's most innovative thought leaders in recognition of their exceptional achievements. As an EDS fellow, Aerdts helps to develop enterprise-wide initiatives that shape the future of EDS. He leads the EDS Fellows Program activities for clients in the communications industry.

Agility by Design

How the Architectural Framework of the Future Enables Leverage and Speed

RENÉ J. AERDTS, PH.D.
ANDREAS G. BAUER
JÜRGEN DONNERSTAG

Executive Overview

Traditional service delivery architectures have become rigid, in that any new service requires major system updates and enhancements. This type of setup does not lend itself to the fast-moving service delivery requirements of Communications Service Providers (CSPs).

The traditional silo-based approach toward service delivery does not support next-generation services and needs to be complemented by systems like the IP Multimedia Subsystem (IMS). In other words, the rigidity of traditional service delivery needs to be replaced by an agile Service Delivery Architecture to achieve speed and leverage simultaneously. That architecture also enables an event-driven environment.

In order to compete in today's fast-moving market of constant innovation, CSPs need to enable event-driven integration, composite application deployment, business service extraction and business process orchestration.

The authors of this paper describe how to design an agile application architecture by applying a set of principles that allows a CSP to achieve both, leverage and speed in its operations at the same time.

Leverage

TRADITIONALLY, INFORMATION TECHNOLOGY (IT) systems have been developed in silos—by line of business, service line, network technology, or operating company—impeding leverage. Application architectures were created in silos (see left-hand side of Figure 1). Often a CSP feels competitive pressure to release new offerings and generate revenue quickly, so it creates ad-hoc systems to respond to commercial drivers.

The CSP then suffers long development cycles, high maintenance costs and slow product launches. In continuing this cycle, the company then finds itself with a collection of disparate systems that are not adequate for a marketplace that shifts from few, highly standardized products to many, highly personalized products (microproducts). In addition to this proliferation of systems, point solutions and vendors impede capitalizing on synergies and create barriers to convergence and global operations.

From Silos to Leveraged Environments

IN ORDER TO COMPETE in the fast-changing telecommunications industry, companies have to enable agility from an applications and infrastructure perspective: a shift to a leveraged environment is required for a CSP to do so (see Figure 1).

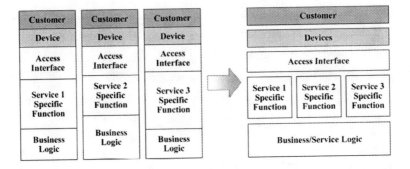

Figure 1 – From a Siloed Environment to a Harmonized Leveraged Platform

Most service providers have committed to this type of approach for reducing capital expenditure (capex) and operational expenditure (opex), and accelerate service time-to-market. Much of the current debate is about the most appropriate technology, the scope of the business benefits and the skills required for success.

The benefits of a harmonized, leveraged platform include sustainable cost reductions, economies of scale and scope, leverage of best practices and best-in-class solutions and enablement of centers of expertise. However, the major reason for a move in this direction is the fact that Operations Support Systems (OSS) solution silos cannot support next-generation services.[4]

Speed

TRADITIONALLY, IT SYSTEMS HAVE been grown organically and business rules and work flows have been incorporated in the code of either homegrown solutions or Commercial Off-the-Shelf (COTS) applications, thereby impeding speed. In essence, the application architectures grown over the last years have created a rigid environment.

---

[4] Gartner. "New Service-Delivery Architecture Require Seamless OSS Integration," July 4, 2006.

In a CSP environment, the typical inefficiencies in this type of rigidity include limited flexibility of tariff plans, workflows and business rules. The resulting environment does not provide the speed required in a marketplace that is characterized by product proliferation; fierce competition; campaigns, designed and executed on short notice; personalized product packages and bundles; and increased complexity of services.

From Rigid to Event-Driven Environments

A SHIFT TO AN event-driven environment is required for a CSP to create the speed needed to compete in today's marketplace (see Figure 2).

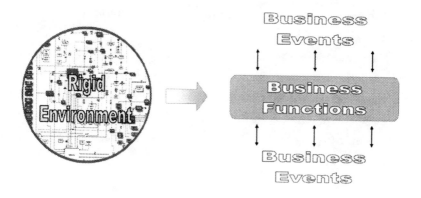

Figure 2 – From Rigid to Event-Driven

Many CSPs have started implementing and realizing the benefits of event-driven architectures. This approach is fully in line with the New Generation Operations Systems and Software (NGOSS) recommendations by the TeleManagement Forum.

The benefits of the move toward a service oriented environment (and the enablement of event-based capabilities that allow for more agility and that are optimized for speed) include accelerated time-to-market, a shift of focus from programming and customization efforts to creating a customer experience, and quick response from customer facing organizations. At the same time, software release cycles are decoupled from changes in product and tariffs. Or, as Gartner[5] puts it: "Today's carriers want an [Service Oriented Architecture] SOA to deliver agility and faster time to market for new communications services and features."

Agility

EVEN THOUGH AGILITY IS something that all corporations want, it is challenging to define and hard to achieve. In our view, agility is defined as the combination of leverage and speed (see Figure 3).

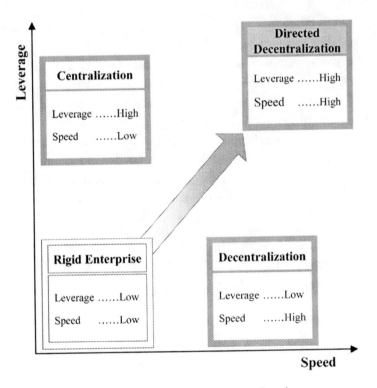

Figure 3 – Agility = Leverage + Speed

---

[5] Gartner. User Survey Report: Carriers' Service-Oriented Architecture and Web Services, June 2, 2006.

Rigidity is similar to entropy. All corporations gravitate toward rigidity over time, as technology ages, systems grow, and system interconnectivity requirements grow. In a rigid environment—characterized by low leverage and low speed—any change to a system or application then creates a spider web of changes that affect other systems. Hard-coded connections then require subsequent updates to linked systems.

There are three possible solutions to this rigidity problem:

Centralization – This approach focuses in centralizing the assets and decision making for the IT resources. The result is increased leverage at the expense of speed. An example of this approach is the mainframe environment, which traditionally is centralized in large data centers: any change is well-coordinated, agreed upon by all constituents, resulting in less-than-optimal speed.

Decentralization – This approach focuses on decentralizing the assets and decision making for the IT resources. The result is increased speed at the expense of leverage. An example of this approach is a corporation with autonomous business units, each with the authority to make IT decisions. The resulting infrastructure is optimized for speed, at the expense of re-usability, resulting in low leverage.

Directed Decentralization – This approach focuses on taking the best from the previous two tactics: allow for decentralization to gain the speed benefit, while centrally setting the tactical and strategic IT direction, resulting in increased leverage. This approach is outlined in this paper.

Lean Operator Program, NGOSS, and the TeleManagement Forum (TMF)

THE LEAN OPERATOR PROGRAM[6] is TMF's flagship program to lead the emergence of lean and agile operators, able to compete in 21st century markets.

---

[6] TeleManagement Forum. NGOSS Release 5.0 Solution Suite Release Notes, RN303, September 2006. TeleManagement Forum. NGOSS Release 5.0 Solution Suite Release Notes, RN303, September 2006. TeleManagement Forum. Telecom Applications Map Release 1.0, GB929, May 2005. TeleManagement Forum. NGOSS Architecture Overview Presentation, TMC1875.

The objective of NGOSS is to guide the evolution of the telecom industry's processes and systems to improve business flexibility and agility. It includes key technical and process enablers, packaged as industry-agreed guidelines like maps, models, methodologies, and specifications.

The objectives for each one of them include the following:

+ Transform operating costs.
+ Transform business agility.
+ Transform levels of customer service.
+ Transform innovation levels.

Core NGOSS Principles

THE TELEMANAGEMENT FORUM RECOMMENDS that New Generation OSS should be based on 10 key business and technical principles of NGOSS:

1. Enable a CSP's business transformation.
2. Reduce IT costs and timescales by utilizing widely available COTS software components.
3. Allow a clear migration path by integrating with and evolving from legacy systems.
4. Reduce software development costs and risks by building on industry best practices and existing standards work.
5. Provide comprehensive, enterprise-wide operational solutions for fixed, mobile, cable and converged industry segments.
6. Allow corporate data to be widely shared across the enterprise and where appropriate with trading partners.
7. Allow the CSP's organization to evolve without systems lock-in by using loosely coupled distributed systems.
8. Allow business processes to be easily changed without software change by separating control of business process flow from application operation.
9. Allow simplified systems integration ("Plug and Play") through clearly defined contract interfaces between applications.

10. Allow simplified systems integration by utilizing a common communications bus between applications.

NGOSS Frameworks

FOUR NGOSS FRAMEWORKS HAVE been defined to guide a CSP through a transformation toward agility (see Figure 4).

- **eTOM** – enhanced Telecom Operations Map[®]
- **SID** – Shared Information/Data Model
- **TAM** – Telecom Applications Map
- **TNA** – Technology Neutral Architecture

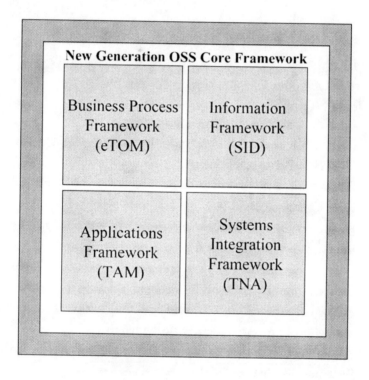

Figure 4 – NGOSS Frameworks

The NGOSS identifies three levels of integration: legacy, today and emerging. Legacy is characterized by poor integration, stovepipe-type solutions and architecture, and inflexible infrastructure, resulting in inflexible service delivery capabilities.

The next level, which we see in today's CSP environments, is characterized by loose integration based on proprietary solutions and products. The architecture consists of multiple databases and multiple user interfaces, which results in an inherent inflexible infrastructure.

The next and emerging level consists of an open and distributed environment, based on components. All elements of the architecture are workflow connected, share data, and are policy enabled. This type of architecture opens up the environment for flexible and rapid service delivery capabilities.

Agility in IT Environments

NOW THAT WE HAVE defined leverage, speed and agility, we can focus our attention to agility in an IT environment, specifically a telecom IT infrastructure. There are four basic qualities that drive agility in an IT environment:

- Knowing what you have, so that when you change it, you know how far the effect will "ripple"
- Knowing how it aligns to business needs, so that as the business needs change, you can quickly assess how the IT systems must change
- Applying effective and consistent standards, so that you know, quickly, how to make any change and can maintain the IT systems with an economic level of effort
- Building on a framework that is designed for change, so that change can focus on the business rules and not on the plumbing

In order to achieve agility, common services should be deployed for those IT components that should only be built once. This approach leads to a layered architecture, loosely coupled integration based on open standards, and reusing and sharing of components.

Traditional Service Delivery

TRADITIONALLY, IN A VOICE-BASED market place, a CSP considers its Operations Support Systems/Business Support Systems (OSS/BSS) core to its service delivery: A CSP's traditional objective was to provide network and bandwidth based services with high levels of reliability and scalability. The delivery infrastructure for network- and bandwidth-centric services is often static and consists of stove-pipe systems, based on co-existence of custom-built legacy applications and more modern COTS products. The required integration and interoperability pose major issues to the CSP (see Figure 5).

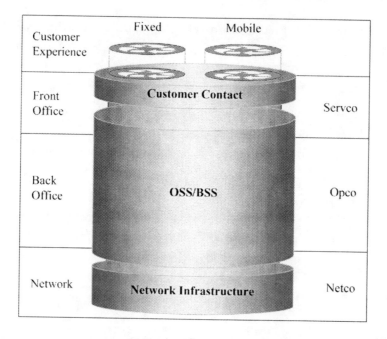

Figure 5 – Traditional Service Delivery Architecture

Agile Service Delivery

AN AGILE SERVICE DELIVERY Architecture, on the other hand, consists of common services across a four-layered, application architecture (see Figure 6).

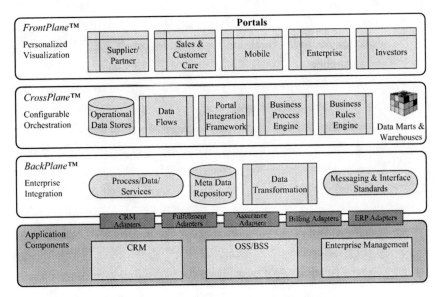

Figure 6 – Agile Application Architecture:
Common Services Instantiation for OSS/BSS

The four layers of this architecture can be described as follows:

Application Components – Provide data and application services and can be implemented through legacy, custom-built or COTS solutions

BackPlane™ – Provides the abstraction needed to insulate the rest of the application environment from changes in point solutions

CrossPlane™ – Provides the mechanisms to modify business processes, e.g. for provisioning (also provides real-time access to data of the operational data store and data warehouse/data marts)

FrontPlane™ – Provides a seamless customer experience across all customer touch points

The key attributes of the Agile Application Architecture (see Figure 6) are as follows:

- **Speed and Flexibility** – Achieved through loose coupling of software assets, which allows the systems to change rapidly to

reflect business process changes or respond to disruptive business
events

- **Flexible Orchestration** – Based on an event driven architecture
  that enables reduced cycle times for decision making and
  interaction with customers, suppliers, employees, etc.
- **Reduced IT Costs and Timescales** – By utilizing existing
  application investment and widely available COTS software
  components
- **Simplified Integration** – By utilizing a common communications
  bus between applications
- **Separation of Concerns Into a Layered Architecture** – Allowing
  the architecture to accommodate changes in technology over
  time, without requiring a rip-and-replace of the entire business
  solution
- **Built on Open Standards** – Supporting a rich and well-managed
  vendor ecosystem and encouraging the inclusion of best of suite
  COTS solutions
- **Secure Sharing of Data Assets** – Allowing corporate data to
  be shared widely across the enterprise, and where appropriate,
  with partners
- **Protection of Previous Investments** – By wrapping and reusing
  existing applications, thus allowing a smooth transition over
  time

Compared to many other innovations, this change is not driven by
technology. Business leaders and lead technologists have been requesting
this kind of change for a long time.

Agile Application Architecture for Next-Generation Services

THE CURRENT SERVICE DELIVERY Architecture needs to be
enhanced to support next-generation services. These next-generation
services include, among others, IP-based services, application services,
content services, information services, multi-media services, fixed-mobile
converged services and advertising.

The Service Delivery Architecture for next-generation services expands the current architecture, which is optimized for network and bandwidth based services.

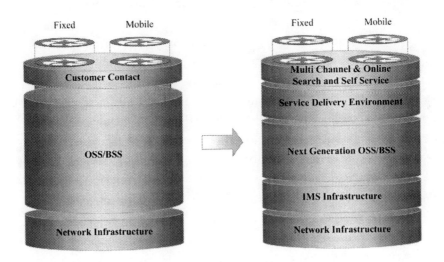

Figure 7 – Agile Service Delivery Architecture for Next-Generation Services

As shown in Figure 7, the Service Delivery Architecture for next-generation services adds two crucial components: a Service Delivery Environment and an IP Multimedia Subsystem (IMS). This approach is in line with a CSP's objective to provide converged services, allowing end-users access to video, data and voice services seamlessly, regardless of the living or working environment. Additionally, this architecture enables a platform for delivery of services, independent of type of service and access technology.

Next Steps

CSPS NEED TO ASSESS the current situation of the IT infrastructure and determine which of the following migration paths make most sense from a mature and end-state perspective:

Enable Event-Driven Integration – The integration of existing applications is reduced and brought under control by using an event-driven, enterprise integration platform. Adapters are introduced at each point of connection, to transform data to and from a common (vendor-neutral) event model, reducing the inter-dependence of the applications upon one another.

Enable Composite Application Deployment – Once the BackPlane™ of the composite application framework is in place, it can be used to host temporary adapters to expose the business functions embedded in the existing applications. These can be consumed to build new, composite applications within the common FrontPlane™. Typically, this drives "quick wins" in customer and partner portals. It is also usual, during this stage, to draw out a number of shared technical services, such as identity and access management. These may evolve from relatively simple beginnings, as the possibility to realize their full value unfolds.

Enable Business Service Extraction – Using an enterprise model of business process automation, the core business functions that are embedded in the existing applications are brought out as shareable "services," further simplifying the integration. This also brings benefits in greater visibility of business activity, as opposed to technical activity.

Enable Business Process Orchestration – The final stage introduces a business-aware CrossPlane™ that captures the data relating to business activity, correlates the data into a holistic view of the business and applies the cross-application rules supporting business level governance.

Conclusion

LIKE MANY OTHER INDUSTRIES, change within the CSP environment is occurring at an ever faster pace. In fact, change no longer occurs at a steady pace; it is happening at an accelerated speed. At the same time, customers are demanding new services that push the current CSP infrastructure to the limit.

The traditional silo-based approach toward service delivery creates a rigid delivery environment, incapable of delivering these types of services at the speed and price that the consumer needs. As a result, a CSP need to move toward an agile Service Delivery Architecture to achieve speed and leverage. This change will give the CSP an event-driven architecture and environment that will allow it to respond to changing business needs.

The forward-thinking CSP will position itself pro-actively in this market and create and implement an event-driven architecture. A CSP that is first-to-market with this type of architecture will be able to serve its customers better, thereby increasing the client satisfaction, and ultimately the Average Revenue per User (ARPU).

About the Authors

René J. Aerdts, Ph.D., is an EDS fellow. He is part of the Information Technology Outsourcing (ITO) Service Delivery organization, which is responsible for the IT component service delivery. The title of EDS fellow is awarded to the corporation's most innovative thought leaders in recognition of their exceptional achievements. As an EDS fellow, Aerdts helps to develop enterprise-wide initiatives that shape the future of EDS. He leads the EDS Fellows Program activities for clients in the communications industry.

Andreas G. Bauer is the global leader of Communications Industry Frameworks in EDS Portfolio Development. He has over 18 years of experience in business consulting and technology enablement, including careers with IBM Global Services, Deloitte Consulting and Dr. Göhring & Partner Management Consultants. He specializes in marketing and IT strategies, process design and reengineering, IT planning, and management of system implementation projects.

Jürgen Donnerstag is a chief architect with the EDS Europe, Middle East and Africa (EMEA) Communications Industry organization and member of the EMEA Architects' Office. He is responsible for providing consistent architecture guidance and support to communication projects and proposals across Europe. He has more than 14 years of experience in developing applications, integration and enterprise architectures. His current area of special interest is service oriented architectures for the communications industry.

Shared Services in Telecommunications

How To Improve Quality and Economics of the Back Office

HARVEY R.A. STOTLAND

Executive Overview

Communications Service Providers (CSPs) face a market that is increasingly globalized and consolidated, where growth is shifting from voice- to data-centric services, and where astute service providers are seeking ways to streamline and strengthen every aspect of their operations. In this climate, CSPs can no longer afford back-office processes that are expensive, disjointed or less than efficient.

After the reengineering efforts of the 80s and 90s, purely driving efficiencies by single process in the back office no longer provides significant business benefit. Also, driving such efficiencies does not necessarily support the next-generation business models that CSPs are espousing. Fortunately, a practical and implementable Shared Services Center (SSC) model has now emerged that supports these new businesses.

The author describes how CSPs can apply the shared services concept to manage Human Resources (HR), Finance and Administration (F&A), and Procurement department activities. He discusses various shared services models, transformation paths and requirements and how CSPs can leverage this approach to reduce costs and drive new efficiencies.

Changes in Telecommunications

A NUMBER OF POWERFUL trends are affecting how a telecommunications company manages its back-office operations.

While voice remains the largest single source of revenue for most CSPs, that traditional business is saturated in many markets. At the same time, consumers have sometimes been slow to embrace and use mobile data, broadband and other data-centric content and applications. The industry is driven by globalization and consolidation, and the need for a CSP to leverage its legacy infrastructure and invest in new services.

In this climate, CSPs must focus on reducing overhead, labor and other operating expenses. Many now struggle to streamline and integrate business support functions across sectors, lines of business and operating units, while at the same time improving the ability to meet service quality expectations.

On the other hand, globalization and post-merger integration have created significant opportunities to drive efficiencies and synergies.

That is why a growing number of CSPs are considering the SSC model. Forward-looking CSPs now see an opportunity to reduce costs and improve both quality and operational efficiencies, through a shared approach to administrative enterprise processes.

Challenges in Administrative Enterprise Management

ADMINISTRATIVE ENTERPRISE MANAGEMENT TYPICALLY includes HR, F&A, procurement and other supply chain functions. Unfortunately, many CSPs struggle to deliver those vital services in an effective and cost-efficient way—a way that takes account of the fact that the CSP is no longer simply operating a network asset business but is in fact engaged in providing content, applications and voice services. Administrative operations are vital to the mission of a next-generation CSP. For example:

- Getting the right skills in place at the right time and in the right (on- or offshore) location with a flexible workforce is an HR issue.
- Managing the cash flow associated with an extended ecosystem of suppliers/ partners to build and deploy content for end consumers is an F&A issue.
- Acquiring network elements just in time to meet maintenance requirements for in-building coverage for an enterprise is a procurement/supply chain issue.

Few CSPs have fully leveraged the advantages of automation and self-help solutions, a situation that drives up support costs and hinders the resolution of basic organizational issues. Limited access to key information often increases "hidden" costs within business departments, while inadequate systems can reduce both cash flow and the efficiency of service to employees and other constituencies. Badly integrated systems can produce bottlenecks and poor communication, while limiting the organization's ability to find and leverage economies of scale.

Isolated and poorly monitored processes can also encourage costly purchasing and capital expenditure (capex) decisions. Inadequate HR capabilities can contribute to less-than-effective training, higher personnel costs and workforce attrition.

In most CSPs, the most basic objective is to reduce costs while maintaining an appropriate level of service quality. CSPs see the benefit of applying globalized, standardized processes across various businesses and geographic regions. They want improved lines of communication, more agile and effective decision-making, and the ability to leverage the organization's best capabilities, regardless of location. CSPs are also looking for these processes to add to the strategic direction of the company. A shared services approach to enterprise management processes can help.

A Shared Services Approach

MANY LINES OF BUSINESS in a CSP—such as wireless, wireline and Internet or broadband services—need and use many of the same basic administrative processes.

In some cases, a single activity affects what traditionally were separate and distinct processes. A travel expense transaction, for example, affects both HR and F&A systems. In other cases—such as contact management and help-desk activities, as well as with IT functions such as application development and management or workplace management—most if not all functions and services can logically be shared across processes, geographies and lines of business.

In a shared services environment, a CSP can reap optimum saving and efficiencies by addressing as many processes and activities as possible in an integrated, optimized way. In many cases, the sharing of staff, facilities and processes is not prohibited by statute or regulations, as such sharing might be in other aspects of a business.

Sharing allows the company to optimize and harmonize processes that are similar across businesses and locations. Sharing reduces redundant work and creates efficiencies, and those improvements can significantly reduce overall costs. By introducing automation and other process improvements, and by spreading those tools across the enterprise, CSPs can also empower employees and enhance productivity. A CSP can use this kind of shared innovation to drive decision making toward the front line, and to add value to a wide range of enterprise management as well as front office transactions.

Shared Services: Approach, Scope and Quality

A SUCCESSFUL TRANSFORMATION TO a shared services model will include the reengineering of processes and applications, so that the CSP can better meet organizational and market demands. By identifying and leveraging opportunities to share systems, applications and infrastructure, CSPs can generate cost synergies, enhance the effectiveness of how these processes support the business, and move management operations to a more strategic level that helps the CSP in its changing business model.

The transformation must address the scope of services to be shared, the required level of quality, and the appropriate model for service delivery.

A CSP can define the scope of a shared services opportunity by first evaluating how many common processes currently exist in the HR, F&A and procurement activities. A good scope analysis will also consider commonalities across lines of business and geographic locations. This evaluation should examine whether a proposed shared solution is large enough to generate the needed economies of scale, potential legal constraints, and the required level of customer/employee interaction. Finally, a good analysis will also evaluate how technology can be applied to deliver improved performance and/or reduced total cost of operation.

When considering a shared services approach, CSPs should also define the level of quality needed in the affected activities. This quality review should address both discrete functions such as general ledger and fixed assets, as well as end-to-end processes such as order-to-cash or purchase-to-pay.

CSPs can drive quality improvements by strategically selecting processes for a Shared Services Center. The quality and cost-efficiency of transactional processes, for example, can often be greatly improved in a shared environment. High-end strategic and planning processes, conversely, are less likely to be located in an SSC.

Alternative Service Delivery Models

SEVERAL MODELS HAVE BEEN developed for the SSC. When compared to efforts to optimize a traditional, stand-alone department, any one of these shared models can deliver improved efficiencies, cost savings and effectiveness in supporting the enterprise. A CSP should consider its specific business situations and appetite for change when evaluating alternative Shared Services Center models and delivery mechanisms.

Center of Excellence SSC Model

IN THE CENTER OF Excellence model, a separate and specialized organization is created to provide process-specific excellence to all lines of business and geographies in the enterprise e.g. one for HR, one for F&A and one for procurement/supply chain. This approach can measurably reduce costs, but requires close management of key competencies and trust between the various lines of business.

Cluster SSC Model

IN A CLUSTER MODEL, multiple organizations are created to deliver common processes to each line of business. The Cluster model can harmonize these processes, but cannot fully exploit the opportunities to reduce costs in a more comprehensive shared services environment.

Virtual SSC Model

THE VIRTUAL MODEL IS defined by a decentralized organization that serves all lines of business and geographical locations. The Virtual approach encourages improved communication in a CSP business and can yield measurable sharing and synergy efficiencies. For some CSPs, the Virtual model can serve as an interim step toward a more comprehensive shared services solution.

Full SSC Model

IN THE FULL SSC model, a centralized organization provides HR, F&A and procurement solutions to all lines of business and geographical locations. While more complex to plan and implement, the Full SSC approach leverages a wider and more complete range of efficiencies and synergies (see Figure 1).

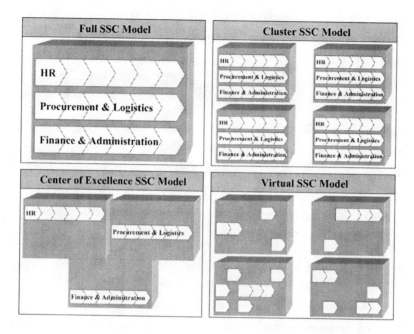

Figure 1 – Alternative SSC Models

Delivery Mechanisms

IN ALL SSC MODELS, the CSP must decide which elements are promising candidates for outsourcing, which could potentially go offshore because of the level of interaction with the business, and which are strategically vital to the future of the business. These trade offs between costs and business agility will help in planning both transition and operation to the Shared Service Center model of choice.

CSPs will also map these enterprise management requirements against current and future service requirements, costs, service overlap/ redundancies, business/IT structures, risk tolerance and investment capacity.

An HR Example

A TYPICAL HR DELIVERY model would address four key layers:

- A self-service capability for employees and managers

- A manned capability for resolving issues for managers and employees
- A strategy function to set policy and business rules
- A layer of supporting applications, data and infrastructure for business support

Migrating to a Shared Services Center model could include the following:

- The development of a multi-channel arrangement to deliver comprehensive HR services to executives, managers, employees and others. These channels include a Web portal incorporating Web-based self-service, e-mail and chat access, Interactive Voice Response (IVR) self-service, fax, phone and traditional mail. It also includes management information and dashboards. The multi-channel arrangements ensure that HR remained in high touch, where required, while focusing on cost management and event-driven processing in repetitive tasks. It also ensures that retained HR professionals focus on strategic issues.
- The development of a mixed onshore-offshore strategy for a wide range of HR services—including payroll, benefits and pensions, compensation, recruiting and staffing, workforce development and workforce administration—to reduce costs and ensure quality. The SSC would provide reporting and metrics, legal support, fulfillment and distribution, accounting and reconciliation and an employee service center.
- The standardization of processes across lines of business and function, in addition to the consolidation of facilities.
- The provision of IT services, such as networking, hardware, applications, security and data warehousing, on a shared and optimized basis.

Companies can apply similar shared services strategies, with appropriate refinements, to F&A and procurement operations in the CSP environment.

Deploying Shared Services

An Implementation Approach

WE RECOMMEND THE EVOLUTION toward a Shared Services Center approach for CSPs, using. a five-step implementation approach to the delivery of shared services:

1. **Baselining and Benchmarking** – Involves understanding current costs, performance levels and the opportunities for outsourcing and service sharing.
2. **Analysis** – Examines the potential path forward, including both in-house and external reengineering and the establishment of future cost and performance objectives.
3. **Transformation Design** – Involves the assessment of the technology infrastructure, the designation of geographic sites for SSCs, the setting of governance processes and any needed contract negotiations.
4. **Transformation and Transition** – Involves transforming the operations into the Shared Services model, including process management, documentation, Enterprise Resource Planning (ERP) application configuration, and transformation management.
5. **Operation and Improvement** – seeks to generate continuous and sustainable improvements in cost savings and overall service performance. This is done on an ongoing basis.

Transitional Pathways

CSPS SELECT AN APPROPRIATE transformational path, based on the CSP's business and market requirements, opportunities and need for change.

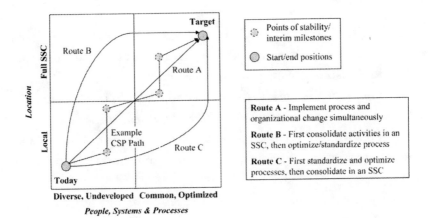

Figure 2 – Pathways to Shared Services

The CSP can take any pathway from its current state toward an SSC environment, but generally, one "axis" leads another for certain periods of time—either lags location process, or process lags location.

Benefits of Shared Services

THE SHARED SERVICES APPROACH can yield measurable advantages for virtually any CSP. A shared model promises financial benefits that a CSP can reap as soon as it begins the transformation, and these benefits accelerate as the organization leverages additional efficiencies. Through economies of scale, the elimination of redundant work and the use of automated self-service technologies, the shared services approach can significantly reduce total cost of operation in the CSP environment.

CSPs can also leverage this shared model to enhance operational efficiencies, to strengthen supply chain management, and to improve the quality and immediacy of reporting and decision making. Companies can also use a shared services approach to improve overall employee satisfaction and productivity.

Conclusion

IN DIRECT RESPONSE TO the competitive nature of the telecom marketplace, companies now seek to improve the quality and economics of their administrative enterprise management operations.

An important new model—the SSC—allows CSPs to better support HR, F&A, and procurement/supply chain activities. At the same time, a shared approach to these important support functions can measurably reduce the total cost of operation across lines of business and geographic sectors.

To capture the benefits of this shared services strategy, CSPs must undertake a fundamental transformation effort. That effort requires the reengineering of administrative enterprise management processes, the use of outsourced and onshore-offshore resources, and a commitment to continuous and sustainable improvements in performance.

About the Author

Harvey R.A. Stotland is a client industry Executive within EDS Global Communications Industry. He has over 16 years in management and IT consulting, systems integration and outsourcing experience, including careers with IBM, A.T. Kearney and Hewlett-Packard. He specializes in business performance improvement, product strategy and implementation, IT strategy, architecture and planning and in the management of IT-based business transformation programs.

The Data Center of the Future

Adapting to 21st Century Customer-Driven Demands

RENÉ J. AERDTS, PH.D.

Executive Overview

Technology is changing at an ever faster pace. Unlike in the past when technology could be deployed for technology sake, it is now imperative to deploy technology based on business drivers and needs. As a result, companies that are able to closely align business and technology will have a competitive advantage in the market.

With virtualization technologies becoming mainstream and adoption rates rising, the Traditional Data Centers have transformed into Virtual Data Centers, where technologies are virtualized to provide business services. Although this trend will continue for a few more years, leading-edge companies are positioning themselves for the data center of the future.

The data center of the future no longer focuses on technology only, but instead it concentrates on the services that need to be provided to the clients. In effect, the data center transforms into a Services Data Center.

The author describes the transformation from traditional, via virtual, to the Services Data Center, with special emphasis on the business impact of this transformation. In addition, the inherent technology, and the associated impact on Communications Service Providers (CSPs), are also covered.

The Future of Data Centers

THE DATA CENTER OF the future consists of a service-driven organization in full support of the business environment. As such, the infrastructure consists of reusable hardware and software components that are provisioned and assembled in real time, based on business needs. For the duration of this business need, the Information Technology (IT) components remain intact, and when additional business needs arise, more IT resources are contracted. At the end, these resources are de-allocated and returned to the IT resource pool for future use.

From a technology perspective, the key drivers for IT change include mobility and convergence. Mobility enables the work force to access corporate information at the right time, in the right format and at the right place to enable the right decision-making. Convergence, on the other hand, is an enabler for this type of interaction with the enterprise, while at the same time slowing down this process, as technologies need to be integrated to provide the end-to-end capabilities.

The data center of the future will intrinsically support these types of capabilities from an integrated point of view. The key enablers for a data center that supports mobility and convergence include service orchestration and service insight. Whereas service orchestration deals with the allocation of IT resources in support of business functions, service insight provides a view into the IT world from a business perspective.

Service orchestration allows for the cost-effective allocation of IT resources to support the business needs and requirements of an enterprise. This allocation requires the creation of service levels that transcend technology and that provide a hybrid view of technology and business, in the form of orchestration of services across all IT components.

Service insight provides a similar hybrid technology and business view of the enterprise. This insight provides an abstraction of business rules that are codified and reused, while enabling an enterprise-wide view of business functions and supporting IT component, based on the viewer's role and context.

IT automation has to move at the speed of business, even as business is moving faster on an almost daily basis. A company can attain and sustain this speed of automation only if it embraces standards at the IT, process, and data center levels. For example, consider Radio Frequency Identifiers (RFIDs). These integrate with an enterprise-wide asset inventory that reflects corporate IT hardware and software assets in real time—to track, manage, allocate and de-allocate assets as business needs arise.

In summary, the data center of the future will be a highly automated, digital nervous system for the business. It will carry out resource and workload placement dynamically to sustain new business development and to reduce operating costs of the business and IT as a whole. For a CSP, this need for change translates into the need for horizontal applications. To allow flexible and instantaneous growth, a CSP needs to invest in IP Multimedia Subsystem (IMS) solutions and utility-like infrastructure implementations.

The Drivers for the Data Center of the Future

IN ORDER TO UNDERSTAND the data center of the future, we need to understand the drivers for change in corporate environments. Some of these major business and infrastructure drivers are shown in Figure 1. It is important to note that some of these drivers overlap from the business arena into the technology area and vice versa.

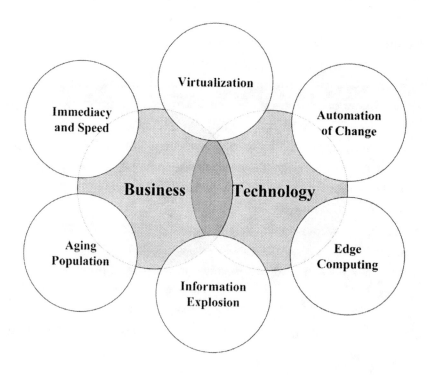

Figure 1 – Business and Technology Drivers

To determine the impact on the data center in support of the infrastructure and the business, we need to have a solid understanding of each driver.

Virtualization

VIRTUALIZATION IS THE METHOD by which functionality and management of servers, storage and network are lifted away from the physical hardware implementation. This separation allows the different hardware types to be treated as a single pool of processing, storage and network resources, defined and governed by policies, service levels and price. Virtualization of resources is a key mechanism used by enterprises to create agility[7]. In order to increase speed, corporations are creating virtual enterprises to bring products and services to market faster. This

---

[7] Agility is defined as the combination of leverage and speed.

virtualization often occurs in conjunction with a merger or an acquisition that a corporation may use to expand its business.

For CSPs, the virtualization needs to occur at all levels of the infrastructure, including the network level. Only through this type of virtualization of all resources will a CSP be able to leverage its installed base, provide end-to-end capabilities and allow for flexible growth at a competitive price point.

Immediacy and Speed

IN THE PAST, IT was good enough to wait for information to be brought to the end user, as reflected in the reports that were usually printed in batch processes and delivered overnight. However, in today's fast moving market, information must be delivered to the knowledge worker at the time the information is needed to make the business decision. Although speed and immediacy are important, the greatest benefit is derived from an integrated business and IT view of the end-to-end process.

For CSPs, being first-to-market requires flexible and adaptable IT and network infrastructures that can instantiate new services at a moment's notice—enabled not only by virtualization technologies, but also a service-oriented approach toward infrastructure and application. Only through the combination of these types of technologies can a CSP roll out and bill services quickly and successfully.

Aging Population

ALTHOUGH THE DATA CENTER is usually not focused on the characteristics of a population or work force, it is important to consider the aging workforce when planning a data center of the future. As the traditional mainframe work force has been employed for over 40 years, the first wave of this generation is getting ready to retire. Although this may not seem like a major impact on data centers, in effect it is. As the younger-generation workforce has grown up in a more open environment, it will shift the focus of new application development toward a more open and standardized environment. A stratified open environment is depicted in Figure 2.

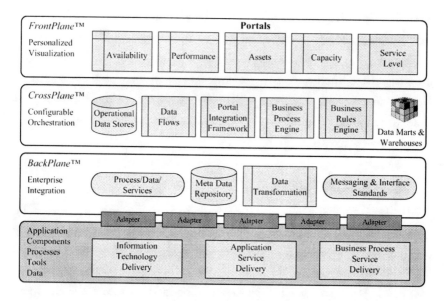

Figure 2 – Stratification of IT in Support Business

The Point Solutions exist at any layer of the environment: applications, information technology and business processes. To extract information from these point solutions in support of the business, an enterprise integration model needs to be put in place to capture and consolidate the information from the various solutions. This task is accomplished in a layer referred to as the BackPlane™, consisting of the adapters for the different enterprise systems. The next layer of abstraction consists of the configurable orchestration layer, also referred to as the CrossPlane™, which is comprised of all the business logic and business rules, as abstracted from the point solutions. This setup makes it possible to leverage the rules and make them independent of the underlying product set. And last, but not least, the end user experience in the form of personalized visualization is provided through the FrontPlane™. This layer visualizes data in separate views, based on defined roles.

For CSPs, this approach calls for the implementation of an IMS-like model, which moves from a vertical and silo application and service delivery arrangement to a more horizontal and leveraged approach, as shown in Figure 2.

Information Explosion

ACCORDING TO RESEARCH BY the University of Berkeley in California, by 2000, mankind had created the equivalent of 12 exabytes of information. In an updated study published in 2003, the analysis showed that the average data growth in new information stored was 30 percent between 1999 and 2002. This explosion of data growth[8] continues and is driven by six major factors (see Figure 3).

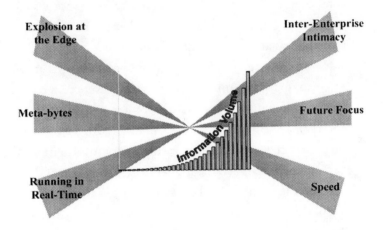

Figure 3 – Information Explosion

1. The first is the movement to real time, or rather "running in real time." It is a transition that started with mainframe batch processing and is accelerating today as companies understand the value of "now." It is no longer good enough to manage data in real time; it also needs to be available in real time so that business decisions can be made based on the most current information. This leads the way for real-time simulation.

2. The second contributor to the information overload is referred to as "meta-bytes," which is information about information. It is the opportunity to understand the "where," "why," "who,"

---

[8] Yuhanna, Noel. Forrester."Trends 2006: Database Management Systems," November 29, 2005.

etc., about the information now being gathered. The key drivers for the growth in interest in metadata include the importance for enforcing enterprise-wide data retention policies, locating and retrieving data in a business-relevant matter in the future, optimization of the physical infrastructure due to growth, as well as semantics and objects in context.

3. The third trend is represented by the explosion at the edge, where data and transactions originate. The embedded technology revolution has begun, and it is populating our world with computational devices so small that they are not visible to the naked eye. Yet, each of these devices has the potential of sending information at unprecedented levels.

4. A fourth driver is the exchange of information with others in the value chain. Maintaining a "four walls" restriction on customer and supplier information is no longer a viable option. Inter-enterprise intimacy is about understanding your customers, their customers and then their customers' information. You also have to understand your suppliers, their suppliers and then their suppliers' information. Those corporations that are able to make use of this information (including metadata associated with that information), will be in a better position to capture market share in the growing virtual enterprise market.

5. The fifth force is information that moves us from the present to the future: the future focus. The type, source and form of information that provides a strong indicator of the future vary significantly from traditional corporate information. This is one of the most interesting new flows of information. And this is exactly where simulation forms the cornerstone of success. Those corporations that can filter through the available information and come up with a winning market strategy will be the forerunners in this new market.

6. And finally when enterprises have the same amount of available information, the distinguishing factor becomes the ability to process it faster and faster. By performing the analysis faster, enterprises basically enable the processing of more data into

information in the same time frame to enable more focused market opportunities. Increased speed of business decisions, more accurate and quicker reporting of financial assets, and improved visibility into operational processes all require faster and deeper information flows.

For CSPs the information explosion translates to the ability to provide customized service to each individual subscriber, based on the consumer's needs. This type of interaction calls for a detailed knowledge of consumers and their interactions with the rest of the world. In effect, we need to understand the complete value chain from supplier to consumer. This interaction is routed through the CSP, which in turn can use this knowledge to customize services. Unless the other components outlined above (virtualization, intimacy and speed, and stratification) are put in place, this type of customization is not possible.

Edge Computing

THE EDGE IS DEFINED as the point where data and transactions originate. In the past, data and transactions could only originate through human intervention. Now, both people and "things" can create these transactions and data. At the same time, the access pattern has changed.

In the old world, people created data or information, and people consumed them. In the new world, things create and consume a majority of data and information—enabled by global connectivity through a global secure network (see Figure 4).

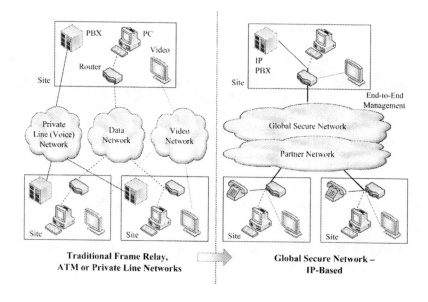

Figure 4 – Global Secure Network and Convergence

For CSPs, edge computing is the paradigm shift that drives all the changes in the industry at the moment. Only through the use of these novel approaches to optimize the use of the installed infrastructure will CSPs be able to survive and thrive in this new world.

Evolution of Data Centers

TAKING INTO ACCOUNT THE business and technology drivers (as shown in Figure 1), the evolution of the data center can be described. This evolution progresses from the *Traditional Data Center* to the *Virtual Data Center*, leading to the *Services Data Center*. At the moment, the transition to the Virtual Data Center is in progress, with different levels of implementation.

What drives these changes? First of all, there are technology changes, in the form of four immutable laws: Moore's Law[9], Gilder's Law[10], Areal Density Law[11] and Metcalfe's Law[12]. The results of these laws, as well as the increased automation capability in the data center, allowed for servers to proliferate outside of the data center. The second driving force behind these changes is business. As discussed, speed is critical to make the right business decision in a timely fashion.

At the moment we can distinguish three classes of data centers (see Figure 5). Of course, there is the *Traditional Data Center*, where servers, operating systems and applications enable the environment. The next level is the *Virtual Data Center*, where infrastructure components (servers, storage and network) are virtualized, with connectivity between the virtualized components enabled through a separate middleware layer. The third type of data center is the *Services Data Center*, where the focus is on business services, with a utility environment enabling these services in a transparent manner.

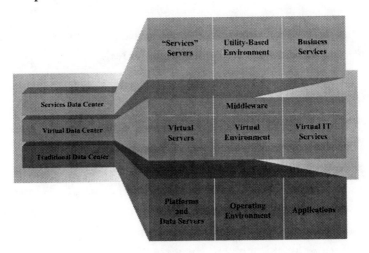

Figure 5 – Data Centers: From Traditional to Virtual to Services

---

[9] Intel Corp. 2005. Moore's Law 40th Anniversary.

[10] Pinto, Jim. Pinto's Point: The laws of technology. The Instrumentation, Systems and Automation Society, 2001.

[11] Kobler, Ben and Hariharan. The Premier Advanced Recording Technology Forum (THIC) PC,. 2002.

[12] Pinto, Jim. Pinto's Point: The laws of technology. The Instrumentation, Systems and Automation Society, 2001.

Each one of these types of data centers is described in more detail below.

Traditional Data Center

IN THE TRADITIONAL DATA Center, each one of the infrastructure components exists in its own silo. Integration usually occurs through a point-to-point solution, adding to the complexity of the overall environment. One of the initial advantages of the silo approach was that applications and systems could be integrated quickly through these point-to-point solutions. This siloed approach makes the IT environment more rigid and prevents the IT infrastructure from delivering business functions quickly and efficiently.

The design principle for the Traditional Data Center is "design for peak," in that each individual resource is designed to be able to handle the peak. This approach, while quite effective in meeting application performance objectives, proves to be a costly solution, not only from a capital and operational expenditure perspective, but also from a leverage point of view, as resources are typically not leveraged.

Virtual Data Center

ALTHOUGH THIS STAGE IS referred to as "virtual," there are several characteristics of these types of data centers.

- **Virtualization** – First and foremost, the key characteristic of the Virtual Data Center is virtualization of all IT resources: server, storage and network. Even though the industry focus at the moment is on virtualization of server resources, the focus will continue to shift toward the virtualization of all IT resources. From a storage perspective, the industry focus is in Information Lifecycle Management (ILM). In the Traditional Data Center, storage was provisioned, allocated, managed and monitored at the application level "Managed Storage," (see Figure 6). The next phase of maturity of ILM focuses on lifecycle management of storage resources at the individual application level, "Information Optimization." In the ultimate stage, all applications are viewed at the integrated enterprise level, allowing for storage management at the enterprise level ("Business Optimization").

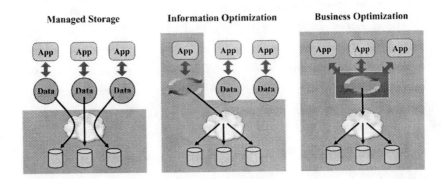

Figure 6 – The Move Toward Storage Information Lifecycle Management

- **Standardization** – It is only through the use of and adherence to industry standard tools, processes and procedures that true integration can occur to enable IT to support the business. If standardization is not present in the IT infrastructure, integration becomes cumbersome, expensive, and prohibitive in rolling out new products and services in a speedy fashion. In this first stage of true standardization at the IT level, the following design principles for the Virtual Data Center are contemplated:

- **Open Plug-In Architecture with Well-Defined Interfaces** – There are a number of standards to select from, but to take advantage of common new functions and to enjoy a plug-and-play capability at the infrastructure level, CSPs must adhere to open standards. Through this capability, business functions and services can be provisioned faster, enabling a business-driven go-to-market strategy.

- **Integration** – An end-to-end management and control capability is critical to optimize the use of these resources. As change transcends limits of the traditional IT infrastructure resources and expands into the business-level processes and events, integration of business and IT becomes a vital component of the monitoring and management capability. As automation penetrates the area of change, integration of IT and business components becomes a given for enterprises wanting to succeed in the speed-to-market game.

The design principle for the Virtual Data Center is "design for leverage," in that all resources are pooled together to be leveraged from an enterprise perspective. This approach provides the design-for-peak-processing benefit of the Traditional Data Center, while leveraging capital and operational investments.

Services Data Center

DURING THE NEXT STAGE of data center evolution, the focus will shift from IT-based resources to business-based resources. Several technologies that currently are in existence or development will aid in this data center transformation. First of all, resources should no longer be considered application-level resources, but rather enterprise-wide resources. This shift in focus requires an enterprise-wide virtualization of resources. At the same time, standardization in conjunction with virtualization, optimization and management allows for resource optimization across the enterprise.

- **Service Orientation** – The key component of the data center of the future is business services. IT is an enabler for business functions, while business functions are consumed as services by clients. However, for this services-based approach to become reality, CPSs must translate current business functions into business services, and map business services to the underlying IT and telecommunications components. This process should be automated and visualized.

- **Virtualization** – From a storage perspective, in the Services Data Center, the focus is on end-to-end transparency. Transparency can drive the increased automation of provisioning, installing, managing, monitoring and decommissioning storage resources. However, in the Services Data Center environment, this is no longer good enough. Data classification should also be automated from an ILM perspective.

- **Standardization** – It is only through the use of and adherence to industry-standard tools, processes and procedures that true integration can occur to provide IT with the speed needed to respond to the ever-changing business needs. These standards are based on the following Services Data Center design principles.

- **Resilience to Changes Over Time** – As changes will continue to occur at smaller intervals and with greater frequency, the overall IT infrastructure needs to become resilient to change. More precisely, the environment will become adapted to change, and the capability to absorb change is incorporated into every IT component.

- **Event-Oriented Digital Nervous System** – In a Services Data Center, the focus is on the services, or rather the events that define the services. Although services need to be monitored and managed, it is the events that the monitoring and automation engines need to act upon. Through this interaction at the event level, monitoring and management is performed at the lowest level possible from a business perspective.

- **Service Oriented Interface Bus** – In order to enable a free flow of information between point solutions, an enterprise-wide interface bus is needed to provide an interconnect between all systems. However, this bus needs to enable the intelligence at the business level to allow service orientation, in that the IT components can be connected with the business services they support.

- **Self-Executing Predictive Monitoring and Control** – In a Services Data Center, a time lag between problem occurrence and resolution is no longer acceptable. In fact, as enterprises start running in near real time, the monitoring will move from reactive to predictive. This predictive monitoring analyzes IT systems trends from a holistic perspective and predicts the most likely component to fail, before this failure occurs.

- **Optimization** – Optimization in the Services Data Center is a direct result of the management and automation capabilities included at all levels of IT and business processes. Optimization in a Services Data Center includes the removal of latency from these business processes.

- **Availability** – Availability is one of the key characteristics of the Services Data Center. In fact, availability is no longer simply a requirement; it is an inherent function of the services provided. Through the use of standardization and virtualization, high-availability solutions will be created on the fly, and additional IT resources will be allocated as business needs arise.

- **Data** – From a storage perspective, transparent data movement and backup will provide the ultimate Continuous Data Protection (CDP). In conjunction with the ILM capability, continuous data availability will transcend technology and move into the business realm by providing business context to data and information.

- **Operations** – In the Services Data Center, the focus is on business services. As such, all operational processes need to not only be streamlined, but also tightly aligned with the business processes. Any change or problem in the operational area can have a broader impact on the overall business.

- **Management** – The management of the overall environment will continue to improve through automation, optimization and several technologies such as utility computing, grid computing and virtualization. However, the process management tools that are put on top of these technologies are the key to enabling enterprises to take advantage of these advances from a business perspective.

- **Business-Driven Automated Change** – Change systems in the past were designed around normal behavior and change was viewed as a disruption. In the data center of the future, normal behavior will be highly automated and those who can derive value from recognizing the exceptions will clearly have the advantage. This "business by wire" or "game of business" capability should allow the enterprise to respond effectively and consistently to situations.

- **Service Levels** – In the Traditional Data Center, service levels are based on traditional IT metrics, such as server availability, online response times, batch windows, etc. As is well known, even if an outage occurs, these technology-based service levels can be met, while there is a severe impact to the business. For that reason, in the Services Data Center, the focus has shifted to business-directed service levels (see Figure 7). A business-directed service level is a service level that measures business metrics, such as meeting billing cycle windows or percentage of provisioning orders completed within specifications. Specifically, these service levels provide an insight on how the business performs.

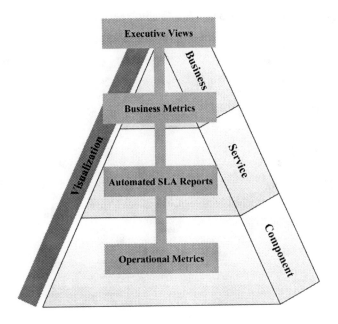

Figure 7 – Transformation from Technology to Business Service Levels

- **Automation** – In the Services Data Center, automation will take a more forceful approach to manage the infrastructure components.
- **Provisioning** – As hardware and software procurement may take weeks (and in some instances even months), in a service-oriented enterprise, it is critical that provisioning of IT resources is automated. This requirement implies that resources need to be available at the time they are needed: a utility model that goes beyond the "pay-as-you-go" concept and incorporates the "grow-as-you need" model (also referred to as the grid).
- **Workload** – The workload component consists of three major areas: breakdown, placement and appliances. The workload needs to be broken down into smaller components than can be executed on the grid. These granular components need to directly tie to business functions or events. As these business events are encapsulated into workload components that get executed on the grid, the automation engine can take action based on events that are directly related to business events. In effect, an event-enabled monitoring capability is created (see Figure 8).

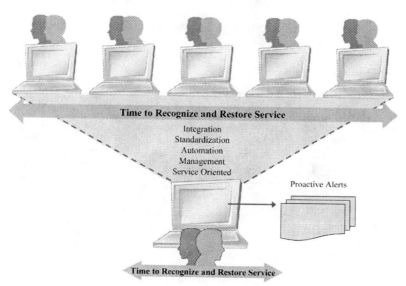

Figure 8 – Event-Enabled Consolidated Integrated Monitoring Console

The next step in this process is the workload (or component) placement: an orchestration engine (responsible for prioritization and placement of the workload) identifies and provisions the best suited IT resources to accommodate the business events, based on the business needs.

And last but not least, as business evolves and matures, business events will be combined into "work roles" within an enterprise, comprising business events with similar characteristics.

- **Integration** – The third element of automation is integration of the individual IT components to allow end-to-end visibility at the enterprise level. Integration also refers to correlation at the data level, such that IT events can be correlated in real time. This setup allows for increased automation capability, resulting in improved problem resolution time.

- **Operations** – As mentioned before, the focus of the operational components is on the business. As such, all processes are geared toward reducing the time to identify and restore services[13]. Through business and IT integration and automation, services can be restored on alternate IT components, thereby restoring service before the original hardware or software components are fixed. In effect, we are moving away from fixing problems in near real time to providing an instantaneous workaround and fixing the problems asynchronously. At this stage, the shift from Virtual Data Center to Services Data Center has been completed.

- **Visualization** – Although management of the IT infrastructure remains key to delivering services, the visualization of these services and associated business service levels becomes an integral part of service delivery.

Traditional service levels will continue to be important from an operational perspective. For that reason, service visualization will perform a mapping of traditional IT (and telecommunications) resources

---

[13] Please note that we do not state "time to identify and restore hardware or software component failures."

to business functions and services. Through this mapping, traditional infrastructure metrics can be obtained and subsequently translated into the associated business functions to assess and visualize the impact to these services. This approach enables a single measurement, allowing for consistency of reporting.

The characteristics of the Services Data Center are outlined in Figure 9. The IT infrastructure is driven by the business in the form of event, services and workload roles. Across all of these components, virtualization, monitoring, management, automation and integration provide the basis for the Services Data Center.

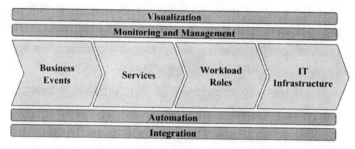

Figure 9 – Integration of Business and IT in the Services Data Center

Table 1 summarizes the required transformation journey from the Traditional Data Center to the Virtual Data Center, leading to the Services Data Center.

Business Scope	Traditional Data Center	Virtual Data Center	Services Data Center
Focus	Information technology	Shift to processes and business	Business and services
Resources	Dedicated	Dedicated and virtual	Virtual
Monitoring and Management	People	Automation	Automated automation
Enterprise Visualization	IT views	Unlinked business and IT views	Integrated business and IT view

Table 1 – Transformation From Traditional to Services Data Center

Business Scope	Traditional Data Center	Virtual Data Center	Services Data Center
Disaster Recovery	Add-on	Transparent	Integral
Orchestration	Ad hoc	Policy-based	Business-based

Table 1 – Transformation From Traditional to Services Data Center *continued*

Impact on Communications Service Providers

THIS TRANSFORMATION FROM THE Traditional to Services Data Center will have a significant impact to a CSP and its overall operational activities. First of all, the traditional IT and network operational areas will become more and more integrated to define a "telco infrastructure," which from the consumer's perspective is "the network." In effect, CSPs will move forward with the convergence model, as this is the only way to create a truly unique customer experience at optimized price points.

Only through this type of integration can we achieve the business service levels (that transcend the traditional IT and network infrastructure) that will drive the services that consumers are buying, as we are moving from a supply-driven market to a consumer-driven market. In the near future, consumers will buy the devices that will enable them to buy the services that they want. This behavior drives the need for CSPs to become service-driven organizations, supported by service data centers, consisting of an integrated IT and network infrastructure to provide the end-to-end services for consumers.

As consumers and enterprises continue to expand their sphere of influence, a tighter integration across platforms, systems, and devices is needed. This can only be accomplished successfully through integration of the different support and delivery infrastructure components, as well as standardization.

Those CSPs that realize this vision and move forward with initiatives like IMS to provide consumers those services that they really want, position themselves as survivors and leaders in this ever competitive market.

Conclusion

TO BE SUCCESSFUL IN the 21st century, a CSP needs to adapt to changing market conditions and customer demands faster than ever before. The company's underlying and supporting infrastructure needs to move at the same, or even faster, pace.

The data center of the future no longer focuses on just technology. It concentrates on the services provided to its customers. The data center of the future basically transforms from an IT-focused center into a service-focused center where delivering superior service to its customers becomes the priority.

This kind of data center transformation is necessary to remain competitive in the telecommunications industry. It requires careful thought and planning because there are specific steps that a company needs to take to get there. A CSP that can make this kind of data center transformation, in a way that is seamless and transparent to its customers, has the ability to thrive in today's and tomorrow's demanding marketplace.

About the Author

René J. Aerdts, Ph.D., is an EDS fellow. He is part of the Information Technology Outsourcing (ITO) Service Delivery organization, which is responsible for the IT component service delivery. The title of EDS fellow is awarded to the corporation's most innovative thought leaders sin recognition of their exceptional achievements. As an EDS fellow, Aerdts helps to develop enterprise-wide initiatives that shape the future of EDS. He leads the EDS Fellows Program activities for clients in the communications industry.

The Workplace of the Future

A Commodity or Means To Improve the Customer Experience

Andreas G. Bauer
Harvey R.A. Stotland

Executive Overview

A new generation of edge devices is changing the nature of the communications industry. To remain competitive, a Communications Service Provider (CSP) has to deliver a new set of services on converged computing, communications and entertainment-edge devices. As a result, the CSP must redefine its own workplace services and strike a balance between delivering quality workplace services fast and reducing its operating costs. These dynamics require a broader set of competencies between a CSP and its partners in order to share in market success. To develop these competencies, a CSP needs to transform both its Information Technology (IT) and Product Management organizations.

The authors describe the market forces that drive the push for a more capable workplace and how CSPs can create a cost-efficient workplace environment by applying automation, mobility and personalization. They also discuss the challenges and opportunities presented by the growth of edge devices and the steps CSPs are taking to capitalize on this trend to improve the end-user experience.

Focus on the Customer

TODAY'S COMMUNICATIONS LANDSCAPE IS marked by a need to reduce costs in an increasingly distributed environment. Much of the logic and the data needed by corporations and by consumers now reside on desktops, smartphones and other devices moving on the network edge.

With the accelerating convergence of communications and computing, devices are increasingly sold by CSPs, and these devices provide access to voice, data, workplace/homeplace, entertainment and other services. To support those new devices, and in response to the pressures of cost and convergence, CSPs need a more comprehensive and efficient approach to workplace management that takes into account both the internal customer, the employee, and the external customer.

In this environment, a forward-looking CSP is working to transform itself into a more agile, customer-focused enterprise. In many cases, single-product companies are evolving to offer multiple services, such as a mobile CSP that now seeks to deliver fixed/mobile or computing/communications convergent services.

To succeed in this migration, a CSP must differentiate itself in an increasingly crowded marketplace by creating and delivering a superior customer experience. The ultimate goal, of course, is to build sustained customer loyalty and revenue growth by establishing itself as the preferred provider in the marketplace.

A Competitive Workplace Edge

SO HOW DOES A CSP position itself to succeed in this customer-centric environment?

A CSP can begin by establishing for itself a managed workplace that is more than a commodity, and that improves its own cost base. As the workplace becomes more complex—due in large part to the proliferation in the number, type and complexity of data-centric edge devices—service providers must respond by deploying more robust and capable workplace management solutions.

A truly successful workplace management initiative will improve reliability by enabling CSPs to do the following:

- Deliver current service levels without interruption.
- Reduce capital expenditure (capex) and operating expenditure (opex) and realize immediate payback.
- Accelerate the deployment of applications, patches and new productivity technologies.

The development of several assets is essential to this initiative. Those include the following:

- A consistent and robust process architecture for the fulfillment, assurance and billing of the workplace to the end customer, plus the management reporting against this process
- An automated, trusted service delivery architecture encompassing data center, servers and multi-device workplaces
- An order-to-cash applications architecture to support the range of personalized workplace services likely to be used by internal and external customers

Those workplace management assets can provide superior cost economics, a prerequisite to compete successfully in a competitive marketplace. Thus, the immediate focus is on reducing capital and operating expenditures, increasing the speed to deploy new applications and upgrades, and delivering agreed upon service levels in a reliable way without interruption.

Creating the Managed Workplace

TO CREATE A TRULY agile workplace, a CSP must align its infrastructure to its business goals. It should also seek to drive increased productivity by delivering end-user edge services in a reliable, secure and cost-effective way.

A comprehensive workplace solution, crafted to meet the specific needs of the communications industry, will address these key requirements:

- **Trusted Infrastructure** – The provision of secure, reliable and available multi-network-based service provision, support, backup and recovery with access to the advanced data services required by the end customer
- **Operational Process Automation** – For self provisioning, role-based deployment, software and patch packaging and distribution
- **Support Services** – A help desk delivered through single-point-of-contact service, multi-level support and reporting, plus field services with on-site and dispatched staff, operating system automation, printer support and automation
- **"IT as a Business" Transformation** – Following an established transition process and by applying ISO 9001 standards (model for quality assurance in design, development, production, installation and servicing by the International Organization for Standardization)
- **Integrated Processes & Tools** – With service request, incident management and workflow based on Information Technology Infrastructure Library (ITIL®) standards.

Workplace services must continue to evolve to meet end customer and CSP needs. Going forward, a crucial goal is to increase the number of supported edge devices, while managing the growing diversity of edge devices and their complex interaction with e-mail, database servers and other periphery devices.

Having introduced automation tools and embraced mobility, the next phase of workplace services will see the deployment of increasingly personalized user services, enhanced asset lifecycle management, new collaboration tools and optimized infrastructure solutions. In the coming years, the workplace of the future will integrate end-user productivity tools such as presence, unified messaging and self-healing capabilities, increased virtualization, enterprise integration and the network intelligence needed to support Voice over Internet Protocol (VoIP) and other capabilities.

To prepare for this more capable workplace of the future, CSPs can adopt a strategy that adds and enhances value through automation, mobile computing and personalization (see Figure 1).

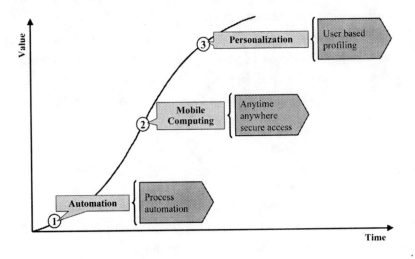

Figure 1 – Strategies To Create the Workplace of the Future

Automation

BY REDUCING THE COMPLEXITY of IT and creating business value, automation removes systemic inhibitors and frees funding to be applied to more productive uses.

Automation requires the application of tools designed to reduce the need for human intervention, thus reducing cost, improving reliability and optimizing overall service capabilities. Automation should be applied to every aspect of deployment and management, including procurement, distribution and provisioning, user help, troubleshooting and repair activities. When applied in a logical manner, this initial transformational step should address consolidation, re-architecting, virtualization and other operational and engineering strategies.

An automated help desk, for example, can leverage a Web-based service core to deliver comprehensive, single-point-of-contact support for enterprise and custom applications, troubleshooting, remote desktop management and technical support, and a wide range of workplace-related business services. In the area of field services, an integrated managed services approach can include expert hardware maintenance including failure exchanges and refurbishing and redeployments, desk-side software support and on-site technical resources.

CSPs can reap substantial and immediate benefits from automation. Those advantages can include fewer help-desk calls, higher resolution rates without need for desk-side support, fewer field-service dispatches and the targeting of on-site support to only the most complex or critical events.

Mobile Computing

BY SUPPORTING GREATER MOBILITY, a CSP allows on-the-go end subscribers and its own employees to create an individualized workplace that fits their personal and professional requirements. To deliver true mobility, a CSP must be able to manage multi-channel, multi-technology workplace devices. A CSP can better serve mobile customers by transforming its workplace capabilities to deliver a more consistent and positive customer experience.

That means the ability to deliver and support an ever-expanding universe of content and applications, from voice and video conferencing to Internet and Intranet services, e-mail, Personal Information Management (PIM), messaging, collaboration and enterprise applications. It also means having the ability to support a growing array of devices, from smartphones and Personal Digital Assistants (PDAs) to Internet Protocol (IP) telephones, laptop computers, both thin and thick desktops, retail kiosks and other output devices, all with multiple operating systems. It may also mean the ability to manage the workplace and homeplace on a single device across service levels.

Competing in the mobile marketplace also requires that a CSP has a comprehensive, IP-based data center infrastructure, including servers and storage, content, hosting and monitoring capabilities, security, metering, billing and management functionality. A truly reliable infrastructure will incorporate features such as automated configuration management, fault detection and repair, load balancing and comprehensive backup and recovery capabilities. Mobility also requires the ability to manage connectivity across all types of networks, from wireless and wireline voice to IP-based, Local Area Networks (LANs), Wireless Local Area Networks (WLANs) and WiMAX (Worldwide Interoperability for Microwave Access).

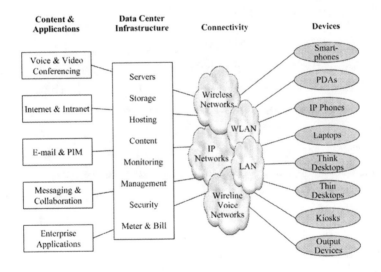

Figure 2 – Mobile Computing

Service providers must manage a growing diversity of multi-channel, multi-technology workplace devices.

Personalization

WITH THE GROWING DIVERSIFICATION of workplace environments and end-user roles that include home and office users, "road warriors," VIPs and third-party customers, the traditional "one size fits all" approach to support simply no longer works. Today's employees want workplace services that are custom-tailored to fit their personal and professional requirements.

To meet those demands, service providers must tailor their tools and services to deliver subscription-based services and to accommodate individualized Service Level Agreements (SLAs). By personalizing services to fit various user profiles, CSPs allow subscribers to access precisely those tools that they really need, and to scale their usage up or down based on personal and professional requirements.

Leveraging the Edge Device

BECAUSE OF THE GROWTH in network data traffic and the proliferation in the type and number of edge devices, support for end-user data devices will be a key requirement for CSPs in the coming years. But as of now, support for data devices remains very much in its infancy.

To deploy, service, and support edge devices effectively in the emerging data-centric marketplace, CSPs must address a number of key business functions. Those include inventory and asset management, system and application configuration, software distribution and patch management, operating system migration, end-user support including help-desk and remote-control capabilities, backup and restore, license management, alert notification and document management.

Furthermore, service providers must now also consider the entire life cycle of a data device, from deployment and configuration through security, tracking, support and retirement. That is why—in addition to its traditional focus on voice services and network management—a CSP is also now viewing content delivery, service delivery and workplace management as integral parts in its overall value chain.

A CSP at a greater level of market maturity also understands that to support data-driven devices reliably, it must address the related issues of workplace connectivity, equipment and software. To do that, it must have the ability to manage customer premises equipment, to deliver field and end-user services, and to manage these technologies throughout their lifecycles.

In a market increasingly defined by the proliferation of devices and IP convergence, the edge device has become a true media gateway for the end user. CSPs now need to manage fixed edge devices such as IP phones, Set Top Boxes (STBs), gaming consoles, home servers and business routers, multimedia enabled phones and even MP3 players. IT-centric devices, such as desktop and laptop personal computers and tablets, when enabled by 3G and 4G technologies, now also require a higher level of support and management.

To compete in the mobility marketplace, where edge device support once meant managing smartphones (e.g. BlackBerry®, Treo™) and other PDAs, service providers must also address the gateway function of a vast new universe of devices.

An IT-Centric Approach

AS THE TYPE AND number of edge devices grows, and as those gateways are sold to millions of new home, small business and enterprise subscribers, the traditional telephony-oriented approach to workplace management is simply no longer sufficient.

While many of these new devices are not overly complicated, they fit and must function in an increasingly large, dynamic and complex network environment.

CSPs can now leverage the robust competencies of the internal workplace to manage this even more dynamic and complex workplace, leveraging the data-oriented platforms, architectures and tools to serve the broader world of modern communications.

A growing number of world-class organizations are now adopting this IT-oriented approach to service and infrastructure support by calling on industry partners to provide comphehensive workplace services management. This allows a CSP to focus more clearly on its core mission.

This managed, alliance-based workplace approach can be used to reduce the operational cost of delivering high value services and to launch and manage popular new services. It can also be used to improve both customer satisfaction and Average Revenue per User (ARPU).

Furthermore, CSPs today can deliver increasingly personalized services on a large scale through the application of a Service Delivery Platform (SDP). Today's most capable SDPs are designed specifically to launch and monetize communications services quickly and cost effectively.

CSPs are becoming increasingly aware of the value of partnering with an IT outsourcing partner that can meet the more complex network and support requirements of the evolving communications market.

Conclusion

AS CONSUMERS DEMAND AND use a dazzling new array of communications tools—from smartphones and PDAs to notebooks, desktop Personal Computers (PCs) and retail kiosks—a CSP must prepare itself to support these increasingly diverse and mobile devices. But provisioning and supporting large numbers of more mobile, data-oriented devices in a distributed network environment is a new and daunting challenge for most CSPs.

To meet these challenges, an astute CSP is evolving its supporting environment to become a more streamlined and agile enterprise structure. That transformation begins by leveraging automation to reduce cost and free funding for new investments. It introduces mobility and personalization to drive new services, greater customer satisfaction and higher profitability. At the same time, service providers can now deploy a more robust workplace of the future capable of supporting these new services and edge devices throughout the entire life cycle.

The key to successful edge device management is the creation of a finite set of pre-defined services and solution components, an attractive price point, and a high level of automation.

By leveraging the capabilities of an IT-oriented workplace—incorporating automation, help desk, asset management and other infrastructure requirements—CSPs can meet the challenges of tomorrow's marketplace.

About the Authors

Andreas G. Bauer is the global leader of Communications Industry Frameworks in EDS Portfolio Development. He has over 18 years of experience in business consulting and technology enablement, including careers with IBM Global Services, Deloitte Consulting and Dr. Göhring & Partner Management Consultants. He specializes in marketing and IT strategies, process design and reengineering, IT planning, and management of system implementation projects.

Harvey R.A. Stotland is a client industry executive with the EDS Global Communications Industry group. He has over 16 years of experience in management and IT consulting, systems integration and outsourcing, including careers with IBM, A.T. Kearney and Hewlett-Packard. He specializes in business performance improvement, product strategy and implementation, IT strategy, architecture and planning and in the management of IT-based business transformation programs.

Part II:

Create a Superior Customer Experience

IN OUR VIEW, CREATING a superior customer experience is key to differentiation. This section contains view points on how CSPs can create points of differentiation in a market of commoditized products.

The Contact Center of the Future in Telecommunications

Achieving World-Class Customer Experience While Containing Costs

Alberto Balestrazzi
Andreas G. Bauer
Harvey R.A. Stotland

Executive Overview

Increased competitive pressures are forcing Communications Service Providers (CSPs) to contain costs and improve customer service. To succeed in this environment, CSPs must manage customer experience and lifetime value.

In this paper, the authors outline their vision for meeting those needs: the contact center of the future in the communications industry. The authors also propose a transition program CSPs can use to achieve that vision.

The Need for Change

IN RECENT YEARS, CSPS have grown rapidly and invested heavily in next-generation network roll outs to support further growth. There has also been considerable spending on point solutions for Customer Relationship Management (CRM) and business intelligence, often without the commensurate change in business model. Now, CSPs want to improve returns on these investments by shifting from a network- and product-centric model to a customer-centric business model.

Managing the customer experience and customer lifetime value are keys to success during this transformation. The customer experience spans the entire customer lifecycle—from learning about a company and gaining brand awareness to purchasing its products or services, connecting to and using them, getting support for problems and even terminating service.

A CSP's business- and customer-facing functions must reflect all these aspects of the customer experience, as shown in Figure 1. In this context, delivering capabilities that match each customer's point of view across all customer touch points, helps the CSP sustain customer satisfaction and a competitive advantage. Studies demonstrate that higher customer satisfaction leads to significantly higher volume and profits; while poor customer satisfaction leads to increased costs (primarily of acquisition) and customer churn. Similarly, point solutions that are not guided by an understanding of the customer lifecycle tend to over spend in certain areas, but under spend on critical "moments of truth" where dissatisfaction can lead to costly churn.

Therefore, CSPs should treat each customer touch point, both direct and indirect—but most especially the contact center and the Internet— as a front door to the enterprise. After all, each touch point gives a customer the opportunity to become comfortable with and trust the CSP, or to turn away. In fact, a customer will decide whether or not to do business with a CSP within the first few minutes of the initial encounter. By providing the best possible customer experience across touch points, CSPs can significantly increase customer capture rates and associated revenues.

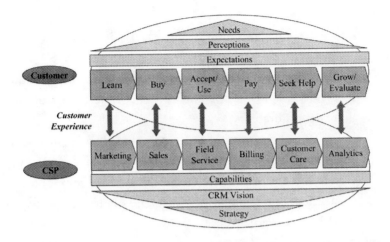

Figure 1 – Matching CSP to Customer Through the Customer Experience

Impact of Communications Industry Trends on Customer Management

GLOBALIZATION OF CSP BUSINESSES, introduction of new service offerings, and efforts to improve Earnings Before Interest, Tax, Depreciation and Amortization (EBITDA) will drive the communications industry in the next years.

- Globalization manifests as:
    - o Harmonization of needs, brands, services, processes and infrastructures.
    - o Industry consolidation through mergers and acquisitions.
    - o The increased willingness of CSPs to form alliances— through which they share concepts, research and development investments or marketing investments, as well as joint go-to-market costs for particular offerings.

- The development of new service offerings is critical to the industry:
  - o Markets are becoming saturated in traditional businesses (voice).
  - o Existing new data services (mobile data, broadband services, applications and content) have been slow to reach profitability.
  - o CSPs are attempting to de-commoditize the business by bundling basic communications with data services in wireline and wireless to create value-added solutions, by developing triple play offerings and by developing fixed mobile convergence.
- Improving EBITDA is the core metric for these businesses:
  - o There is intense competition from traditional players, cable companies and new entrants, as well as fixed-mobile substitution, leading to price cuts, pressure on margins and flat Average Revenue per User (ARPU).
  - o As a result, CSPs are more willing to share risk and reward with external providers that can provide end-to-end services and commit to business outcomes – with the objective to increase adaptability to external market factors and convert fixed cost schemes into variable ones.

These trends all have huge implications for customer care and billing because of increased service complexity, the drive for commonality of approach for a customer and the intense focus on the costs and return on customer care assets.

To respond to these trends, CSPs are adopting an important strategy: refocusing attention on the customer and aligning business areas to a customer-centric approach. Unfortunately, many CSPs underestimate the implications of change projects that cross process and organizational boundaries—and wrestle with implementation challenges as a result.

Under investing in customer care training and contact centers contributes to the challenges. Benchmarking shows that CSPs typically spend less in these areas than companies in other industries.

In many cases, too much work is coming into the most costly agent-manned channel. The use of self-service or alternative channels, although growing, is still low. And finally, multi-channel integration for most CSPs is very limited. The high numbers of repeat calls and handoffs, along with limited automation, keep transaction costs high. Furthermore, increased product complexity and multi-channel access mean agents must have additional customer care and technology support skills.

Many CSPs try to solve these issues through incremental projects that create high expectations for lower costs, reduced churn or enhanced revenues. Often though, these projects fail to deliver full benefits. One reason is a focus on the "low-hanging fruit" and the subsequent failure to address areas for substantial cost savings and improved capabilities. Another reason is an implementation approach that is limited in scope, siloed or technology-centric. Furthermore, some CSPs place a relentless focus on cost per contact center seat, when a balanced approach to the cost and quality of customer experience might be more appropriate. In some cases, increasing cost per seat (by providing agents with multiple skills, for example) and providing a range of alternate low-cost channels, might improve customer satisfaction and reduce total costs of customer management.

We believe that customer management is not only a critical success factor for a CSP, but also a way for it to differentiate from its competitors. Furthermore, a segmented or micro-segmented approach to customer satisfaction is a necessary prerequisite to achieving profitability by segment at optimum cost. As globalization and consolidation gain momentum, standardized processes and technology tailored to localized tariff and regulatory requirements are critical for ensuring a best-in-class customer experience.

Increasingly, CSPs are looking to achieve these business goals in four areas:

- **Organizational Agility** – Additional capacity provided on a flexible basis helps CSPs handle forthcoming revenue generation/ retention campaigns, e.g. data product cross-selling and up-selling, corporate product introduction, or higher technology migrations (handset upgrades to take advantage of 3G-enabled services). Such flexible capacity also makes it possible to reduce the staff needed for peak loads. In addition, to retain knowledge and customer intimacy while avoiding the costs of up-scaling and downscaling, CSPs must manage a complex in-sourced/ outsourced, full-time/part-time, onshore/offshore workforce.

- **Process Excellence** – CSPs are learning that brand can be protected in an outsourced environment, that customer care is a core function but may not be a core competence and that access to best-in-class processes is essential. These processes include multi-channel contact center management integrated with provisioning; network operations and maintenance; billing; business intelligence; distribution channel management; marketing; sales management; and customer retention, termination and winback.

- **Technology Excellence** – CSPs need to drive out costs quickly by using technology improvements that leveraged outsourcing providers already have in place. Then, CSPs can drive business to automated channels, improve efficiency, and generate and protect revenue by linking managed analytics and contact centers. Outsourcers are typically in a better position to provide these services more efficiently than a CSP can.

- **Commitment to Results** – Outsourcing providers should be able to support or commit to results in customer satisfaction, revenue generation and cost containment. Providers who have deep contact center and industry expertise have become more sophisticated in developing working arrangements with CSPs that commit to outcomes.

The Contact Center of the Future

CSPS CAN TURN THE contact center into a differentiator and effectively balance three key business goals (see Figure 2). By using the transformation approach described in this paper, CSPs can achieve a contact center of the future:

- **Contain/Reduce Costs** – We recommend handling certain complex transactions at a manned contact center while moving simple ones to alternative lower-cost channels. This approach takes into account customer lifetime value, micro-segmentation and customer profitability analysis to determine and put in place best practices for handling specific customer segments. It also uses automation and tailored services/channels to minimize errors and handoffs. As a result, CSPs deliver what the customer needs at the first touch point—and contain or reduce costs in the process.

- **Improve Customer Experience** – The recommended approach "inverts the organization" by putting the customer experience at the core and giving customers quick and simple access to value-added processes—facilitated ordering, activation, maintenance and billing—across all touch points. A 360-degree view of the customer, delivered through integrated automated and non-automated channels and the use of real-time common data, helps CSPs identify problems immediately and resolve and handle them consistently. It also improves customer satisfaction and reduces the likelihood of churn.

- **Gain Market Share, Grow Revenue, Retain Customers** – Through an integrated multi-channel customer experience, CSPs can use insights from powerful analytics—including previous contacts, current service usage, competitive analysis and customer feedback—to improve targeted sales campaigns and service/product propositions. This is an effective strategy for increasing service acquisition rates and requests for service changes/upgrades. In addition, all customer touch points have opportunities for cross- or up-selling new value-added data services, migrating existing customers from low-value to high-value products and delivering products and services through an appropriate mix of higher- and lower-cost channels. The goal here is to optimize profitability and lifetime value by customer segment.

Contain/Reduce Costs	Improve Customer Experience/ Satisfaction	Gain Market Share, Grow Profitable Revenues, Retain Customers
• Reduce agent costs by reducing cost per seat, improving training and on-boarding processes and improving agent/manager ratios • Reduce work volume by shedding to automated channels and reducing repeat calls and handoffs • Improve agent utilization through workforce management, staffing processes and decreased contact handle time • Reduce avoidable field service • Reduce collaborative CRM costs • Reduce operational CRM applications and infrastructure costs • Reduce telephony fulfillment costs	• Provide choice of interaction channels to customers • Respond better to individual customer needs (personalization) • Enable a differentiated customer experience based upon customer lifetime value and segmentation • Present a consistent corporate experience to customers across channels • Make product/service recommendations based on historical and real-time behavior, usage or needs	• Improve close rate • Improve up-sell • Improve cross-sell • Improve customer retention of profitable segments • Guide customers by segment to appropriate channels

Manage Performance

Figure 2 – Balancing Goals in the Contact Center of the Future

The contact center of the future matches a CSP's requirements by offering organizational alignment, process management, technology integration and performance management.

Organizational Alignment

CUSTOMER SEGMENTATION IS CRITICAL for improving customer care and developing the most appropriate contact center organization. Of course, customer segments vary in their growth potential, profitability, buying behaviors, typical length of lifecycle, channel preferences and customer service requirements. A CSP, therefore, must carefully determine its customer segmentation, how much budget to allocate to each segment, and which cost structure to apply to serve each segment.

In the contact center of the future, the multi-channel contact center organization serves customers of all segments, prospects and distribution channels in a fully integrated way (see Figure 3). It provides all types of access channels—from traditional voice and mail, fax and e-mail to e-enabled and m-enabled (mobile-enabled) channels—and is flexible enough to encompass new channels as they emerge.

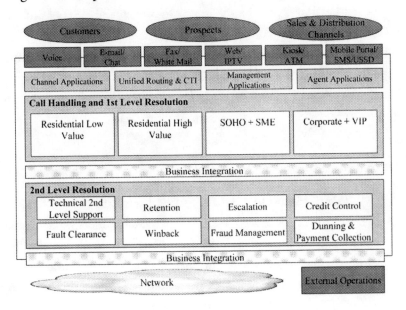

Figure 3 – Integrated Contact Center Organization

How does the manned contact center organization fit into the picture? Our approach is to organize the front office by segment to offer differentiated first-call resolution services, and the back office by specialty and resolution area across segments to achieve critical mass. This approach provides better load balancing, optimized skill usage and lower overall costs. The CSP's front and back offices are seamlessly integrated with one another, with other internal organizations and departments (such as network operations and maintenance), and with outside organizations (such as credit bureaus, logistics operators, and entities managing number plans or geographic information).

Another aspect of the approach is to integrate self-service channels and processes whenever appropriate. This is a way to reduce or eliminate expensive but low-value-added human-handled contacts and to provide customers with additional choices. But we believe that it is crucial to consider carefully how self-service might affect the customer experience before putting the technology in place. Indeed, several types of contacts, such as certain sales contacts, will always require handling by human beings. Furthermore, self-service must align with the CSP's brand and image of customer service.

Finally, the organization's contact centers and sources of supply should be managed as a unified whole, using standardized multi-channel contact center and CRM solutions. This delivers flexibility, scalability, improved infrastructure management and business continuity.

Process Management

THE MULTI-CHANNEL CONTACT CENTER should provide short, clear, effective processes that deliver what customers wants (leaving them satisfied), provide sufficient information for management analysis to tune the next customer interaction, and lead to lower overall cost-to-serve. For this reason, it supports the enhanced Telecom Operations Map® (eTOM), the industry-accepted operating model developed by the TeleManagement Forum.[14] Aligning with eTOM reduces costs by streamlining flow-through processes for fulfillment, assurance and billing. It also improves the quality of the customer experience through its concept of customer lifecycle management—across planning, sales, fulfillment, assurance, billing, retention and service termination.

These processes are supported by an integrated set of tools and applications, as shown in Figure 4 and Table 1.

[14] TeleManagement Forum. enhanced Telecom Operations Map® (eTOM) – The Business Process Framework, Release 5.0, GB921, April 2005.

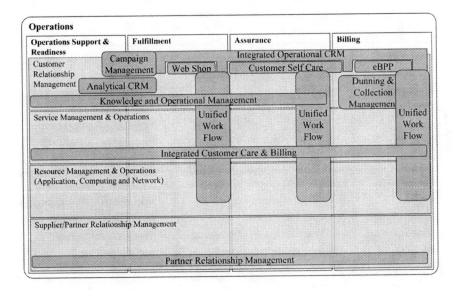

Figure 4 – Selected IT Applications Mapped to the eTOM Process Model

Application	Features	Benefits
Integrated Operational CRM	• Spans fulfillment, assurance, billing • Integrated with customer care and billing (CC&B) • Includes self-service capabilities – Web shop, self care, and electronic bill presentment and payment (eBPP)	• Uses information captured in one part of the lifecycle to improve cross-sell/ up-sell in another • Reduces time-to-service and improves service quality for the customer service representative (CSR) • Reduces cost-to-serve through self-service
Analytical CRM and Campaign Management	• Includes customer, product and usage data • Defines segmentation, propensity to buy, propensity to churn and lifetime value • Allows planning of effective campaigns	• Closes marketing loop and learning from each customer interaction • Uses "market-of-one" data to make actionable choices in operations

Table 1 – Applications Supporting the eTOM Processes

Application	Features	Benefits
Integrated Customer Care and Billing	• Links order to cash • Used for payment collection and dunning	• Reduces time for first payment • Reduces inaccuracy and revenue leakage • Allows collection to be used to improve the customer experience
Knowledge and Operational Management System	• Spans fulfillment, assurance, billing – supported by unified workflow • Gives CSPs a single point of information on competition, customer situation and own products	• Improves quality, speed and richness of response for CSR and Web • Improves customer satisfaction and retention
Partner Relationship Management	• Manages relationship between distribution channel, customer and the CSP • Expands information available to channel	• Makes the CSP easy to do business with • Increases breadth and availability of contacts with the CSP, leading to greater customer satisfaction

Table 1 – Applications Supporting the eTOM Processes *continued*

The overall benefits for process management include improved time-to-market, improved efficiencies in process execution and process duration, reduced error rates, consistent process execution and exception handling, and improved flexibility in process adjustments and process maintenance. And all of this leads to a much stronger customer experience.

Technology Integration

THE TECHNOLOGY OF THE contact center of the future builds a virtualization layer between the channels and features supporting the client, the telecom/network routing layer supporting the contact center, and the agents/management in the contact center itself. The technology embeds management features such as workforce management, quality monitoring, customer analytics and an operational management dashboard. It also provides the agent with features such as operational CRM, business intelligence and a wealth of productivity applications that enhance the customer experience. These features are abstracted from and communicate with the interaction channel through channel and contact management features such as portals, call distribution, routing, and multi-channel automated call handling. Figure 5 illustrates this contact center technology strategy.

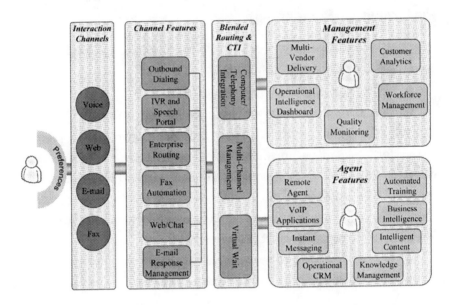

Figure 5 – Contact Center Technology Strategy

The result is a virtual hosted contact center environment that can be turned on or off depending on volume. A CSP can accordingly use several seat providers in several geographies—delivering calls anywhere but keeping the workflow associated with the calls under centralized control. This approach removes large infrastructure costs from the contact center, makes the entire operation more flexible to handle different workloads, and embeds key processes in the network—rather than in the center itself. Centralized infrastructure also helps reduce long-distance charges and isolates changes in contact center structure, contact center technology and CRM applications from each other.

A technology improvement plan that focuses on maximizing cost savings by shifting work to alternate channels, mainly Interactive Voice Response (IVR)/speech portals and the Internet, and by improving call handling and workforce management, enables CSPs to significantly improve Key Performance Indicators (KPIs) such as IVR termination rate, error rates, average handling time and agent utilization.

Performance Management

PERFORMANCE MANAGEMENT AT THE contact center of the future is governed by two simple ideas:
- What gets measured gets done.
- We can only manage well what we can measure well.

We believe that simple efficiency and cost metrics have a place in the performance management toolset—but need to be in balance with customer satisfaction, service quality, revenue protection and generation targets. This balance of goals allows CSPs to improve customer satisfaction, customer lifetime value and customer experience while also lowering total costs of contact center management.

To ensure effective performance management, the approach breaks down KPIs by core processes and channel, such as service activation, reactive churn control, proactive cross-selling, and covers the three dimensions of customer satisfaction, productivity and quality/value-added.

Our approach also defines different service levels for each segment. This ensures that service levels are in line with the brand and image of the CSP, realistic market expectations, and requirements for each customer segment and service type.

To remain competitive in terms of customer service, CSPs must have a plan to improve contact center performance continuously and keep technology in line with what is best in class. Best practices in customer operations give a CSP insight into the ways it can continuously improve and plan for future requirements. One such benchmark, the "Stages of Excellence" study, suggests that contact centers move up quartiles of performance and outcome relative to their peers through continued investment and transformation (Figure 6).

The benchmark provides qualitative and quantitative metrics of comparison within the communications industry and allows a CSP to evaluate improvement over time, including during the course of the transformation. The benchmark itself evolves so that a "Stage 4" CSP is always in the upper quartile of contact center performance.

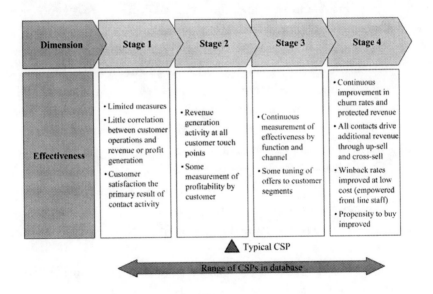

Figure 6 – Example of an Indicator in the "Stages of Excellence" Benchmark

Transformation Program

THE TRANSFORMATION PROGRAM HELPS CSPs meet these organizational, process, technology and performance goals—and achieve a contact center of the future.

Our program is guided by a clear strategy:

- Achieve the lowest possible costs for effective operations without compromising service quality and the customer experience.

- Increase top-line revenue growth.
- Acquire and retain customers at the lowest possible cost.
- Improve the profitability of each customer segment.

The program includes three stages: Improve, Optimize, Transform. Additional upfront analysis helps the CSP understand the related budget requirements and estimated benefits and ensures that contact center performance is fully aligned with the CSP's brand and quality image in the market.

Typically, a full transformation takes between 18–36 months, with improvement and optimization phases taking up to 12 months, depending on the scope and level of integration:

- **Improve** – Activities include standardizing processes; establishing target service levels; implementing performance management; implementing Web, speech recognition and IVR technologies; and reorganizing the contact center around "best customer to best agent." During this phase, selected tasks can move to nearshore and offshore sites.
- **Optimize** – Activities include optimizing alternate automated channels; implementing new CRM, if required; integrating contact center processes through unified workflow; integrating analytical and operational CRM; and optimizing CSR hiring, training and retention programs.
- **Transform** – Activities include achieving a customer-centric agile enterprise business model based on customer-segmented requirements; creating the holistic customer view; and developing customer loyalty programs that reflect real lifetime value.

This transformation approach shifts the balance in the contact center budget away from CSRs to information technology (IT). Analysis shows that the industry lags others in adoption of contact center technologies.

We suggest CSPs implement the transformation program by launching one or more of the following five initiatives:

1. Shift work to alternate channels by:
   a. Developing and improving alternate channels and ensuring that simple processes can be delivered through these channels
   b. Providing multi-channel access capabilities and integrated customer data
   c. Ensuring channels cover the entire customer lifecycle
   d. Improving support for indirect channels
2. Improve call handling by:
   a. Standardizing processes and procedures, scripting and exception handling
   b. Optimizing routing to correct agents who can provide first-call resolution
   c. Enabling information flow and call transfers between front and back office functions
   d. Providing a comprehensive and easy to use desktop environment for CSRs
3. Improve workforce management by:
   a. Standardizing processes for forecasting and daily staff management
   b. Improving automated work distribution across sites, providers and agent pools
   c. Improving quality management tools and metrics
   d. Developing effective on-boarding, training and knowledge management

4. Improve the effective agent wage rate by:
   a. Moving contact centers to cost-effective locations, considering factors such as labor, skills, attrition, and infrastructure availability and cost
   b. Developing differentiated experience by segment and customer value and align agent wages to segment to improve likelihood of profitability
   c. Reducing skill requirements by providing CSRs access to process steps and recommended wording
   d. Protecting intellectual capital of highly specialized and technical staff
5. Improve infrastructure, enabling the other initiatives, by:
   a. Optimizing and consolidating locations of facilities
   b. Centralizing Computer Telephony Integration (CTI), IVR/speech portal, queuing and routing technology
   c. Optimizing operational CRM, interface with account management and billing, and linkage between business intelligence and CRM
   d. Providing a standardized, optimized contact center management suite

To ensure the desired business results from the transformation program, a CSP should work with its transformation and outsourcing providers to obtain commitments to key performance indicators. In addition, all parties must understand the communications industry's products and processes—in addition to its capabilities in business transformation, IT management and contact center management.

Conclusion

CSPS ARE REALIZING THAT transformation to a multi-channel contact center is an important way to provide a world-class customer experience while containing costs. The dynamics of the communications industry, and the relationship between customer satisfaction across the customer lifecycle EBITDA are demanding a different approach to that transformation.

Only an approach that combines a strong guiding vision and best practices, along with business transformation capabilities, operational capabilities and global infrastructure, can provide the desired results. The vision provides a mechanism to avoid the pitfalls of point projects that do not move the customer to the center of focus for the entire organization. Best practices allow a CSP and its preferred providers to work collaboratively to select where to add function and where to remove costs on items that have material impact on the "moments of truth" in customer satisfaction. Capabilities and infrastructure are the base requirements that allow a CSP to generate a return on investments quickly and to help its competitive position.

About the Authors

Alberto Balestrazzi is a client industry executive at EDS for major telecom accounts in Europe, Middle East and Africa (EMEA). He is responsible for innovation, thought leadership and demand creation, and for enabling growth and transformation for clients. He brings more than 18 years of experience in the communications industry. He has worked as a management and technology consultant for major operators across Europe. Balestrazzi has held leadership roles with IBM, A.T. Kearney, Booz Allen Hamilton and Accenture.

Andreas G. Bauer is the global leader of Communications Industry Frameworks in EDS Portfolio Development. He has over 18 years of experience in business consulting and technology enablement, including careers with IBM Global Services, Deloitte Consulting and Dr. Göhring & Partner Management Consultants. He specializes in marketing and IT strategies, process design and reengineering, IT planning, and management of system implementation projects.

Harvey R.A. Stotland is a client industry executive with the EDS Global Communications Industry group. He has over 16 years of experience in management and IT consulting, systems integration and outsourcing, including careers with IBM, A.T. Kearney and Hewlett-Packard. He specializes in business performance improvement, product strategy and implementation, IT strategy, architecture and planning and in the management of IT-based business transformation programs.

Operationalizing the IPTV Environment

Creating a Stable Back-Office Environment To Deliver a Superior Customer IPTV Experience

VINOD KRISHNAN

HARVEY R.A. STOTLAND

TARA L. WHITEHEAD

Executive Overview

Responding to the continued erosion of its core wireline voice business, a Communications Service Provider (CSP) faces enormous pressure to find and pursue alternative market strategies. Now, many CSPs see the emergence of Internet Protocol Television (IPTV), which is launching television over IP networks, as a way to tap the multi-billion dollar pay-television market. This market, long dominated by Multiple Service Operators (MSOs), both cable and satellite, is a way for a CSP to recoup massive network investments and to position itself to "own the home" in the consumer space.

CSPs see and understand the promise of IPTV, but to win in the complex and highly competitive entertainment, communications and information markets, the CSP must deliver the superior customer experience needed to pull subscribers from its current service, typically provided by an MSO, to the new IPTV offering. The CSP must, therefore, address a number of significant challenges:

- Network and business architecture
- Content acquisition and management
- Storage management
- Video and video server management
- Value added service offerings
- Service delivery and back-office integration
- End-user support

The authors of this paper describe the challenges that CSPs face. They also cover the importance of learning how to operationalize the IPTV environment to maximize efficiency and to ensure a top-quality customer experience.

The Next Generation of Entertainment

AS THE CSP WATCHES the continued decline in revenue from traditional voice services and increased commoditization of the industry as a whole, it is seeking new, next-generation service and market opportunities. One very bright spot on the horizon is IPTV. IPTV holds the potential to forever change the television marketplace by revolutionizing the consumer's in-home experience for acquiring information, communications and entertainment services. While it presents a number of complex challenges, this emerging technology has the potential to breathe new life into the fledgling CSP market by opening potential new revenue streams, leveraging key network investments and increasing subscriber loyalty.

CSPs have already begun trialing or planning to trial IPTV, with the initial objective of gaining wallet share from cable, satellite and broadband providers. Because of the heavy dependence on the network infrastructure, managing and maintaining the IPTV environment requires specialized knowledge and capabilities. A CSP who invests in these core capabilities will position itself to exploit fully a growing and lucrative new market.

A 2006 study by Research and Markets[15] forecasts that global IPTV subscriptions will increase from two million in 2005 to some 34 million by 2010, a compound annual growth rate (CAGR) of 60%. IPTV will see its most robust growth in North America, where a CAGR of 78% is expected by the end of the decade. The U.S. pay-TV market generated more than $55 billion in subscriber revenue in 2004[16], and the forward-looking CSP is positioning itself to "own the home" by claiming its share of the emerging IPTV marketplace.

IPTV Defined

IPTV IS A COMPLETE, integrated platform designed specifically to deliver broadcast-quality standard and high definition video and emerging TV services over broadband networks. The transport protocol for IPTV is Internet Protocol (IP), but the quality of service standards require specific service implementations to overlay a private IP network (rather than the public Internet) over high bandwidth-capable infrastructure such as fiber, Digital Subscriber Line (DSL) or mobile broadband provided by a CSP, or even cable provided by an MSO. Due to differences in market conditions and requirements in various global markets, IPTV service implementations can vary significantly by geography, by the bandwidth of the underlying physical infrastructure, and by the selection of technology business partners.

IPTV offers a number of advantages. It allows CSPs to transmit to any connection point willing and capable of providing broadband access, ensuring true anywhere/anytime television service. IPTV

---

[15] The Diffusion Group. Research and Markets. "Subscriptions for IPTV are Expected to Increase by 78% in North America to 2010,"Aug. 28, 2006.

[16] Harris, Amy and Greg Ireland. IDC. "Enabling IPTV: What Carrier's Need to Know to Succeed," May 2005

globalizes television content, gathering TV programming and channels from anywhere in the world and delivering those programs directly to broadband subscribers.

By the nature of IP, IPTV also enables the use of multiple applications simultaneously. IPTV provides a wealth of new interactive and personalization capabilities, such as the ability to select the on-screen view from a variety of available camera angles. CSPs can cater to the preferences of individual subscribers by offering personalized communication services from a variety of media sources. IPTV also supports home media sharing, allowing subscribers to play music and view PC-stored photographs on their television. It is these additional services, coupled with triple and quadruple-play offers that will induce consumers to respond as enthusiastically as they have to pay-TV offers in the past.

Understanding the IPTV Opportunity

FOR CSPS, IPTV REPRESENTS a major move into the world of home entertainment, information and communications. In that highly competitive sector, consumers expect and demand an extraordinary level of service, selection and reliability. TV subscribers have shown a much lower tolerance for service interruptions and a far higher demand for responsive technical support.

To compete against cable, satellite and other key providers in the industry, a CSP will invest billions of dollars to upgrade its network infrastructure to fiber, next-generation DSL, or mobile broadband in order to provide next-generation services to the home—including interactive video services. Most are pursuing a fundamental shift toward the converged network environment in which voice, data and video will be delivered across IP-centric networks to a wider universe of subscribers. But to meet higher consumer expectations in the IPTV space, CSPs must also create and operationalize a customer-oriented business model. It is yet to be proven whether this business model allows CSPs to re-coup initial deployment investments plus the ongoing costs of operational support. This is why developing and executing an operational support plan for wide-spread deployment is an essential part of launching this profitable service.

Operationalizing the Environment

A NUMBER OF CHALLENGES face any CSP that is considering the deployment of IPTV. IPTV requires significant and ongoing product development, because while the fundamental technology for the commercial application of IPTV is now available, significant operational challenges remain:

- **Reliability** – Unlike voice service, where subscribers tolerate a certain level of faults, consumers have shown they have little or no patience for spotty video services. IPTV subscribers often use the service to view live events, during which they expect and demand consistent, high-quality service delivery. For example, if IPTV fails while a consumer is watching an important sporting event, the consumer will lose faith in the technology. A scenario like this is all it takes for the angry sports fan to drop the service and move back to a previous-generation, proven service.

- **Scope of Service** – Consumers require a reason to migrate or take up IPTV service. A CSP must, therefore, build and tailor innovative applications that sit on top of the IPTV platform based on the needs of its target consumer base within its specific markets.

- **Content Choice** – To meet those high-consumer expectations, a CSP forms new partnerships with content providers, at a minimum matching MSOs, but also allows content providers additional reach and methods of further monetizing its digital assets.

- **Customer Service** – The complexity of the service, and in particular the increasing sophistication of the edge devices required to view IPTV, make the provision of high quality, low-cost customer service a major operational issue.

While CSPs have been launching network services successfully for decades, IPTV differs significantly from typical CSP offerings. All the components required are the types of hardware, software and services used by information technology (IT) companies rather than CSPs. Therefore in addressing reliability and scope of service issues, CSPs must develop or acquire a new set of competencies.

Reliability

THE IPTV SOLUTION REQUIRES high availability and strong Fault, Configuration, Accounting, Performance and Security (FCAPS) management processes for all components in the network. This covers every aspect from high-bandwidth infrastructure to acquisition servers, distribution servers, video on demand servers, application servers, storage, and Set Top Boxes (STBs). It also includes the final edge device—the viewing mechanism. The final edge device is likely to be a Personal Computer (PC), mobile phone or Personal Digital Assistant (PDA).

All must be monitored and managed in real time to meet quality of service requirements. A CSP must have the ability to assess, quickly and accurately, where and why a failure has occurred, since any fault could potentially affect thousands of customers. The CSP must also have the ability to diagnose and repair failure of a relatively complex device. This involves working with STBs versus a Public Switched Telephone Network (PSTN) phone at the in-home level across its subscriber base.

In addition, CSPs should establish cost-effective, preemptive maintenance programs across the distributed environment to ensure sufficient capacity and availability to meet customer needs.

Scope of Service

MANY IPTV-TYPE SERVICES EXIST today in the PSTN or existing MSO world. The promise of IPTV is in the seamless integration of these services—the ability to do IP-chat, handle a mobile or electronic commerce transaction, have a voice conversation, share other media, seek further information or watch other TV streams—all while watching the first TV stream appeals to basic consumer needs.

Yet the development, management and integration of applications beyond the core IPTV service implementation—easy to use and personalize to the mass consumer—are still in the infant stage. The CSP now must have the ability to build, deploy, maintain, sunset and re-invent multiple instances of an IP applications environment as quickly as consumers require. This is a very different capability from developing network-based PSTN or Intelligent Network (IN) services, where personalization was limited and service lifetimes were longer.

The challenge for CSPs is to support a very different form of service creation and a different service delivery environment than has been supported in the past.

Content Choice

CONTENT PROVIDERS WILL NOW hold the CSP accountable for the monetization of its digital assets. CSPs, therefore, have a new series of requirements for tracking utilization of these assets, and the associated rights that previously had been the responsibility of others. These requirements will have effects on interfaces and the provisioning, billing and inter-party settlement systems being part of the Operations Support System and Business Support System (OSS/BSS) environment.

Customer Service

THE TRADITIONAL PAY-TV, END-USER environment was relatively simple. In the IPTV world, potentially any IP-capable device could be at the edge, and the applications available to the end user are far more complex. Thus the range of assurance questions and the skill level of agents who provide end-user support must be far superior. Furthermore, automated help systems need to ramp up in coverage and quality.

A Partner Approach for Implementation and Management

EACH ELEMENT OF AN initial IPTV roll out represents a significant challenge for many traditional CSPs, requiring significant IT capabilities in what is seen as a network service. IP clients, servers and storage are deployed into Network Data Centers (Central Offices) and to the edge, requiring design, build, test and operations capabilities core to IT service providers, but peripheral to many CSP network operations groups.

There is, therefore, a partnering opportunity for CSPs to move more rapidly with IPTV service deployment and to bring forward revenue. There is also a similar partnering opportunity for accessing the FCAPS capabilities required to enhance the ongoing reliability of the service. And finally, IT service providers have capabilities in IP application development, digital asset, digital rights and content management, service creation and delivery and order-to-cash integration/enhancement that meet the challenges of launch and beyond.

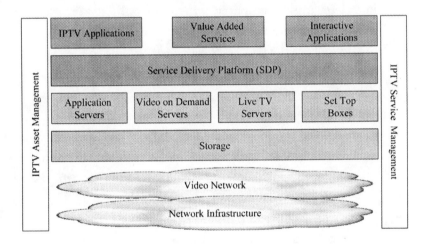

Figure 1 – Complete IPTV Operational Environment

IPTV requires a new stack of infrastructure, from edge devices to servers and storage, in addition to new applications interfaces to OSS/ BSS. It will almost certainly require modifications to the capability of the Service Delivery Platform (SDP). In addition, there will be modifications to business processes for end-user support and internal service assurance (help desk).

Infrastructure Support

PARTNERING FOR INFRASTRUCTURE SUPPORT allows CSPs to take less risk on designing, building implementing and managing IPTV on an ongoing basis. Partnering also improves reliability and performance. Infrastructure support consists of the following:

- **STB Management** – This includes automated software and patch distribution; hardware and software configuration, and asset management; and security management. High-quality STB management processes, technology and tools will ensure optimal performance of the service, reduce errors and reduce customer service calls. By applying similar tools to PC support (e.g. remote monitoring and environment takeover), CSPs can also avoid expenses associated with field service. The numbers of STBs in the environment (potential tens of millions) increases the management complexity so that only highly mature IT service providers have the processes capable of scaling to the challenge.

- **Server Management** – A number of specialized servers are required to run an IPTV network, to support live TV acquisition, instant channel change, video on demand etc. Server management supplies high availability; business continuity services; automated system and application upgrade and patch management; configuration and security management; as well as service assurance monitoring.

- **Storage Management** – Storage requirements for video are huge, so the requirements for high availability, design for performance, content replication, etc. are complex. Storage management supplies proactive monitoring, business continuity services and content lifecycle management.

- **Service Assurance Help Desk** – Troubleshooting the IPTV service requires an end-to-end perspective with multiple technologies involved from the consumer edge device (TV, PC, mobile device), to the STB to the server, storage and IP network. The help desk needs to be re-equipped with the tools, knowledge and processes required to act as a backup to the end-user contact center if required. In addition, the help desk must provide proactive monitoring and management. This type of service assurance is found in a service delivery architecture that is compliant with Information Technology Infrastructure Library (ITIL®) standards and extends across heterogeneous technology types that includes applications.

Applications Support

PARTNERING FOR APPLICATIONS SUPPORT helps configure the service for use, ensuring that services will monetize quickly, assure revenue and provide interest to end consumers, on an ongoing basis. Again, this is core business for some IT services providers. Applications support includes the following:

- **OSS/BSS Integration and Support** – This ensures that the IPTV environment is aligned to provide a simple yet rewarding fulfillment, assurance and billing experience, and that revenue and problem events are tracked between the environments.
- **Service Creation Environment (SCE) Integration and Support** – This is the hosting and management of an integrated Microsoft® .NET Framework and Java™ SCE to support the development and marketing of third-party IPTV services and solutions. The managed SCE should provide tool support in addition to process support from ideation through to market trialing and from potential service release to production.
- **Service Delivery Platform (SDP) Integration Support** – This is the hosting and management of a run-time service orchestration environment that allows tested leaf and composite services to be run on production IPTV. The platform would provide core enabling services to the IPTV applications such as interfaces to other networks and protocols; Authentication, Authorization, and Accounting (AAA) services; identity management; subscriber profiling, as well as platforms for audio/video streaming, gaming, and content editing.

Business Process Support

PARTNERING FOR BUSINESS PROCESS support helps the CSP manage the end-user service experience and improve the core IPTV offer. There are two processes that typically require business process support:

- **End-User Customer Care** – The end user views his personal home device (TV, PC or mobile device) as the edge, or primary gateway back into the CSP's environment, but in reality, end-user customer care will also include the STB. Skilled technical staff will be required, with tools and suitable knowledge, in order to provide care on a wide range of devices and IPTV applications— and potentially on the content as well.

- **Service Ideation To Launch** – Third-party value-added service developers and the CSP will both need process support for Product Lifecycle Management (PLM). These PLM processes should encourage developers and content providers to add unique capability to the consumer's experience. The applications—like interactive games, movies or music—created by those independent software vendor (ISV) players and content providers can be further monetized and increase the stickiness of end consumers to the CSP's service bundle. Operating such an open "sandbox" rather than "walled garden" is only achievable if adequate security, standards and common methods are in place. In addition, the CSP must encourage its ISV community to use the SCE and run testing/implementation at a low cost.

The Promise of IPTV

IN THE PAST, CONSUMERS have fragmented their household spending for information, communications and entertainment (ICE) on multiple providers—specialists in internet-based or physical media distribution. They pay for fixed and mobile voice telephony, audio and video broadcast and personal entertainment. IPTV is the last leg in the ability of many CSPs to provide the "quad play." This would allow CSPs a chance to capture the majority of the ICE household market share and ultimately "own the home."

The rationale for significant network deployment can only be justified by such high bandwidth service that is differentiated against current offers by offering:

- Added-value applications that integrate ICE and content types
- Superior customer care and seamless user experience across the "bundle"
- Reduced costs of the "bundle"

IPTV delivers on this promise. But to leverage the IPTV opportunity fully, a CSP must reach critical mass in the areas of IP infrastructure, applications and business process launch and management capabilities.

Conclusion

BY ADOPTING A PARTNERING approach to launching and managing IPTV service, CSPs can go to market with a solution that delivers comprehensive capabilities, from content all the way to the end-user device. A CSP can thus fully operationalize its IPTV capabilities, with a scalable solution that is supported at the infrastructure, applications and business process levels.

This measured approach allows CSPs to provide an IPTV service that is at least as reliable as existing TV service, provides differentiated applications to enhance the consumer experience, provides content choice and is supported by high quality customer care. Only by providing all four of these will an IPTV service provider encourage consumers to switch or take up service—allowing CSPs to make a return on investment.

About the Authors

Vinod Krishnan is an enterprise architect at EDS with over 10 years of experience in the Communications Industry. He specializes in developing IT strategies and architectures, defining systems integration solutions and creating IT transformation road maps to enable clients to respond to business imperatives. Vinod is currently working on solutions for next-generation data and IPTV services.

Harvey R.A. Stotland is a client industry executive with the EDS Global Communications Industry group. He has over 16 years in management and IT consulting, systems integration and outsourcing experience, including careers with IBM, A.T. Kearney and Hewlett-Packard. He specializes in business performance improvement, product strategy and implementation, IT strategy, architecture and planning and in the management of IT-based business transformation programs.

Tara L. Whitehead is a client industry executive within EDS Global Communications Industry. She has over 16 years of experience in the telecommunications industry and IT consulting, including careers with the Department of Commerce's U.S. & Foreign Commercial Service Division in the Netherlands; IBM Corporation; and IBM Global Services, for Europe, Middle East and Africa. She has spearheaded the IPTV internal taskforce to define the EDS proposition. She also helps clients build capabilities to deliver next-generation services and customer care support. She specializes in next-generation solutions and IT transformation projects.

Part III:

Create Sustained Customer Loyalty and Revenue Growth

WE BELIEVE CSPS NEED an ecosystem of partners that jointly create a superior and attractive customer value proposition, building on the unique strengths of each partner. This section contains view points on the value of collaboration in a converged market.

Revenue Generation for ICT Companies

Creating New Streams of Revenue in a Converged Marketplace – Monetizing Data Services With a "Revenue-Generation Engine"

ANDREAS G. BAUER

TIMOTHY C. SAMLER

Executive Overview

Cost reduction continues to be a key business driver in the communications industry. But forward-looking Communications Service Providers (CSPs) are now getting into a position to compete in the growing and lucrative converged communications marketplace. To do that, CSPs need to make huge investments in new network infrastructures and network upgrades. However, an investment in infrastructure alone is insufficient. CSPs must also find a structured and proven way to monetize services in this new information and communications technology (ICT) environment.

In this chapter, the authors describe the dynamics of a converged ICT market and how companies can profit from the new wave of next-generation technologies to generate a promising revenue stream.

A Changing Market

IN RESPONSE TO THE realities of the marketplace, CSPs have made tremendous efforts in recent years to reduce operating expenditures in networks and in internal organizations. Those efficiency efforts will continue, but service providers are now looking beyond cost reduction to confront a market that offers both tough competition and promising new revenue opportunities.

Change is the one constant of the ICT marketplace. Cable companies are moving into telephony services, cities are deploying wireless networks, CSPs are rushing to deploy "triple/quadruple-play" services and customers are eager to try and buy an exciting new menu of data services such as video on demand and gaming.

Companies that can give consumers the services they want, when and where they want them, and at a competitive price, will reap the rewards of this converged communications landscape. CSPs are poised to invest billions of dollars in new technologies—such as 3G, Fiber To The Curb (FTTC), Fiber To The Premises (FTTP), Next Generation Networks (NGN) and more— in order to exploit this enormous market opportunity.

"According to In-Stat, the 1.9 million U.S. homes passed by FTTP [Fiber to the Premises] in 2004 will increase to 11.8 million by 2009. Assuming revenues of $20 per month, this represents an addressable end-user market of $2.8 billion per year. The total number of homes in the U.S. is 110 million; this represents a total addressable end-user market of $26.4 billion per year."[17]

"The Americas and Europe will ... lead the world in mobile gaming ... U.S. Mobile gaming revenue is expected to reach $1.79B by 2009 with a CAGR of 54% over the years 2004 to 2009."[18]

A CSP can claim its share of this more complex, data-oriented communications marketplace. But to do so, it must be able to create and

---

[17] *Telephony*, April 27, 2005.
[18] White Paper. "Mobile Games," International Game Developers Association, June 2005.

go to market with new services in weeks, not in months. It must develop the systems and processes that create and encourage a true "customer first" culture. The CSP must work to transform itself, often through close alliances with technical and business partners, into a more agile and responsive organization.

Finally, and most importantly, CSPs must adopt a logical, workable and proven way to monetize these next-generation services.

The Challenges of Monetization

DATA SERVICES PRESENT CSPS with significant opportunities to build customer loyalty, new revenues and higher profits. But to exploit these opportunities, CSPs must have Service Delivery Platforms (SDPs) capable of monetizing those services in a rational, cost-effective and predictable way.

A CSP, however, faces a number of challenges in its effort to modernize its organization, to transform its networks, and to create and use revenue-generating SDPs.

These transformation projects are typically very large and complex efforts, and the CSP may underestimate the integration needed to accomplish its goals in a "brownfield" environment. Unfortunately, the CSP often focuses its revenue-generation efforts on a single application or service. While the siloed, architectural model worked well in the past, it is no longer adequate in an environment where services proliferate, and it defeats one of the fundamental benefits of a truly leveraged revenue generation platform. Also, many projects are inadequately funded, mainly because planners do not fully appreciate and communicate the business benefits of a revenue-generation platform.

After installing an integrated platform, the CSP should put in place an organization capable of collaborating with third parties that will provide the services, applications and content needed to succeed in this market.

To maximize its potential in the new converged, data-driven communications marketplace, the service providers should understand the key components that comprise a successful "Revenue-Generation Engine." In addition, success requires that CSPs overcome significant business, technical and execution risks that the transformation journey entails.

The 10 Key Components of a Revenue-Generation Engine

THE REVENUE-GENERATION ENGINE IS made up of 10 key components needed to ensure the success of an ICT revenue-generation program (Figure 1).

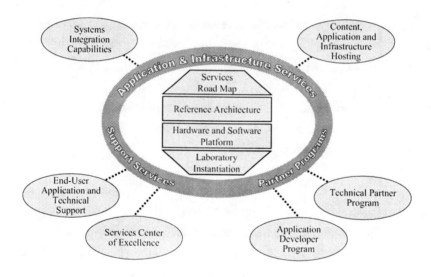

Figure 1 - The 10 Key Components of a Revenue-Generation Engine

1. **Services Road Map** – The first important step in monetizing services is the creation and/or refinement of a Services Road Map. This road map identifies those services the CSP expects to launch within a given period of time, and should be formulated based on market demand and the CSP's underlying business strategies. A good Services Road Map will also be closely linked to the technology road map, and together those two documents are the basic planning tools for a Revenue-Generation Engine.

While most service providers maintain at least the basics of a services plan, a detailed services road map should take into consideration the CSP's existing service and technology mix, customer needs by market segment, competitive pressures and specific service opportunities. A company can use this detailed road map to describe the phased introduction of services—such as gaming, media on demand and other new offerings— and to define and prioritize the network investments needed to open new revenue streams around those services. The services road map drives the requirements for the platform and allows a logically phased build out—thus avoiding the siloed approach.

2. **Reference Architecture** – A Reference Architecture provides the basic technology blueprint that describes the building blocks of a Revenue-Generation Engine. A Reference Architecture should be technology neutral, to allow a CSP to leverage its existing Information Technology (IT) investment fully and to provide maximum flexibility in the selection of hardware platforms, software elements and service options (see Figure 2).

    A logical, well-planned architecture should optimize integration capabilities, thus reducing the effects of network complexity, by identifying common components like services catalog, identity management, Authentication, Authorization, Accounting (AAA) and others. It should allow future components to be installed and launched quickly and easily, and should leverage open standards to avoid locking-in proprietary technologies. The Reference Architecture is, in reality, a functional document, and must encompass the Services Road Map, the release plan and the underlying technologies and support systems needed to monetize those service offerings. A Reference Architecture should be formulated based on a clear understanding of how those vital elements fit into the overall Revenue-Generation Engine.

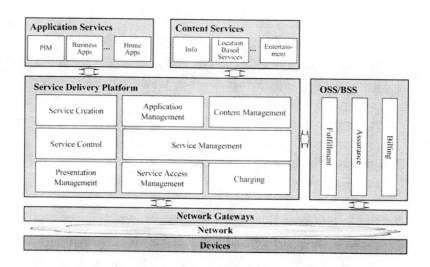

Figure 2 - The Revenue-Generation Engine Reference Architecture

3. **Hardware and Software Platform** – To maximize the revenue generating potential of services in the converged marketplace, the CSP will also need to add certain hardware and software assets to its infrastructure. Those assets should be selected based on the ability to support the Services Road Map and the Reference Architecture, and to contribute directly to the monetization of new services. A good platform will already contain some pre-integrated components, thus reducing the time and cost of deployment.

To ensure optimum performance of the overall Revenue-Generation Engine, the CSP must ensure that the hardware and software components it selects represent best-of-breed solutions. CSPs should seek out those vendors that have preconfigured solutions to avoid "reinventing the wheel" and to save time and cost. Those systems should also enable seamless integration in three key areas: with content provider systems; with the CSP's Operations Support System and Business Systems Support (OSS/BSS); and with current and future network elements. Additionally, the platform must support a powerful service creation environment that will allow the CSP to launch new services rapidly and provide the agility to respond to changes in the market quickly.

4. **Laboratory Instantiation** – Service providers should insist on examining a Laboratory Instantiation of the Reference Architecture before acquisition and deployment. That pilot should demonstrate an end-to-end value chain of the key business functions—including hardware and software, integration and partners—to ensure that the elements of the proposed Revenue-Generation Engine will work as an end-to-end business solution.

5. **Technical Partner Program** – Relatively small, highly specialized vendors will provide many of the technology components and much of the content that CSPs can leverage to open new revenue streams. Coordinating those vendors and technologies presents an enormous challenge, particularly in the new and rapidly evolving converged ICT marketplace. It is expensive, time consuming and difficult to qualify, certify and manage all these vendors individually.

   To address that challenge, a forward-thinking CSP relies on a Technical Partner Program, run by vendors and IT integration specialists. Large software vendors already operate mature technical partner programs that address a wide range of issues, including interoperability, product and staff certification, standards compliance, software developer resources, application programming interfaces and technical and after-sale support. Systems Integrators (SIs) can help coordinate these vendors and ensure all solutions fit seamlessly into the CSP's revenue-generation plans.

6. **Implementation Road Map and Systems Integration Capabilities** – Given the technical complexity of monetizing services in a converged communications marketplace, integration is one of the biggest challenges faced by CSPs seeking to deploy a Revenue-Generation Engine. Service providers can measurably reduce the risk of deploying a Revenue-Generation Engine by working with a proven systems integration partner.

A Systems Integrator with deep IT experience can ensure the Revenue-Generation Engine consists of carrier-grade systems, linked by industry-wide standards for connectivity and interoperability, and backed by reliable Service Level Agreements (SLAs) that guarantee end-user service quality. A good SI will offer a comprehensive suite of professional services and a history of service delivery excellence. CSPs should also expect an SI to provide a comprehensive Implementation Road Map detailing every step of the Revenue-Generation Engine deployment, including, for example, the design, build and implementation of the solution.

7. **Content, Applications and Infrastructure Hosting** – The converged communications market is a dynamic and highly volatile environment. Consumer demand for new services, and the technologies needed to support those solutions, change at a breathtaking pace. CSPs must move quickly to recognize evolving demand, to deploy new applications, and to go to market quickly to capture those emerging revenue streams. That pace of change creates real opportunity for CSPs, but it also translates into significant cost and risk.

To meet the demands of this rapidly changing marketplace, CSPs can now leverage the advantages of the managed hosting model for infrastructure, applications and content. By outsourcing those requirements to a trusted hosting provider, CSPs can quickly deploy new systems and services using "pay-as-you- go" pricing, thereby avoiding significant operating expenditure (opex) and capital expenditure (capex). Often, popular new content or services originate from very small, unproven vendors. By placing those resources with a proven hosting provider, CSPs can deploy cutting-edge solutions with confidence. A service provider can also leverage managed hosting to scale its operations quickly, up or down, in response to fluctuations in demand.

8. **End-User Application and Technical Support** – While most CSPs handle calls well, some struggle with providing application and technical customer support for data-centric services. When

subscribers need assistance with a product or service, they want the problem solved quickly. A less-than-effective help-desk operation can lead to dropped calls, frustrated customers and increased churn.

To deliver superior technical and customer support, many CSPs now rely on experienced IT organizations to provide help-desk services for all products, applications and content. A quality support operation can lower service costs while reducing churn and increasing overall customer satisfaction.

9. **Application Developer Program** – Small independent application developers are creating some of the most popular and profitable innovations in the communications industry. There are, in fact, literally thousands of developers across the globe creating solutions for mobility, entertainment, productivity, content and other applications. Those applications are often the "sizzle" that draws subscribers, and they represent an important element in any CSP revenue-acceleration plan.

But it can be very difficult for a small application developer to bring even a brilliant solution to market. And it is equally challenging for a service provider to sort through the universe of offerings to find the applications that will drive its revenue model. To bridge that gap, CSPs can take full advantage of established application developer programs run by major IT vendors and SIs.

Those programs function to sort through a myriad of potential applications to find the most popular, robust and profitable solutions. The programs then subject those applications to a process of standardization and certifications designed to ensure that they will function smoothly in a carrier-grade operational environment. Software development toolkits give developers access to the enormous market potential of the CSP. And service providers can select from a qualified menu of pre-tested, certified service applications.

10. **Services Center of Excellence** – Once a CSP has developed and launched a Revenue-Generation Engine, it needs a logical

way to govern and monitor this complex go-to-market program. Few providers have built the internal structure and resources needed to manage this complex set of road maps, architectures, technologies, expertise and partnerships. For most CSPs, it makes far more sense to acquire these capabilities—on an as-needed, "pay-per-use" basis—from a proven IT vendor that specializes in those capabilities.

CSPs can call on such a vendor to establish a Services Center of Excellence to provide comprehensive, end-to-end governance of every element of a Revenue-Generation Engine (see Figure 3). This center functions as a services dashboard, showing the CSP the current status and performance of all services and partnerships from both a technical and financial perspective.

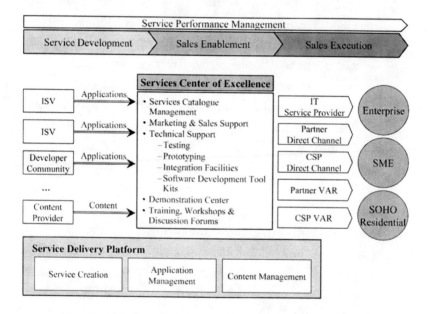

Figure 3 - Services Center of Excellence

Monetizing Services

WHEN SELECTING A REVENUE-GENERATION Engine, CSPs should look for a solution that delivers proven, enterprise-class performance. A reliable solution will provide the following:

- An integrated, carrier-grade SDP able to support all types of data services
- An open, interoperable solution not tied to any proprietary product but that can support both Java™ and Microsoft® .NET Framework and is supported by leading third-party vendors
- A standards-based architecture with OSS/BSS integration capabilities
- Best-of-breed hardware, software and services support, provided by preferred allied vendors
- A proven, pre-integrated solution that minimizes opex and capex
- Global capabilities, including consulting, integration, implementation and support services and automated hosting with utility pay-as-you-go pricing
- Proven multi-year experience with IT services

By focusing on a single, integrated solution, CSPs can avoid the silo approach and create a reliable and highly scalable SDP.

Benefits of a Revenue-Generation Engine

CSPS CAN DEPLOY A proven Revenue-Generation Engine to accomplish the following:

- **Reduce Technical and Execution Risk** – A pre-integrated, standards-based solution that reduces complexity.
- **Reduce Business Risk** – A hosted solution that leverages a global infrastructure, offering cost savings, pay-as-you-go pricing, and reduced opex and capex.
- **Minimize Market Risk** – Includes a service creation environment that enables the rapid launch of new services and the agility to quickly respond to market changes.

- **Access Innovation** – Exploits partnerships to create attractive service offerings comprised of information, entertainment and communication services to increase customer loyalty.

The Approach to Operationalize a Revenue-Generation Engine

THE RECOMMENDED APPROACH TO operationalize a Revenue-Generation Engine covers the entire lifecycle—from an initial assessment to implementation to ongoing operations and management—and comprises of six steps (see Figure 4).

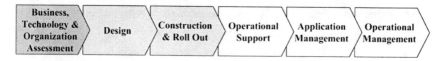

Figure 4 - The Approach to Operationalize a Revenue-Generation Engine

Successful implementation requires a holistic approach that centers on market requirements and that orchestrates the elements of corporate strategy, product marketing, network design, IT and capital investment. To this end, CSPs should employ a proven end-to-end implementation approach comprised of the following six steps:

1. **Business, Technology and Organization Assessment** – Analysis of the current situation in terms of services road map, technology and organization; definition of target state architecture, business case and implementation road map.
2. **Design** – Detailed design and selection of point solutions.
3. **Construction and Roll Out** – Solution built, integration with existing environment and initial roll out.
4. **Operational Support** – Ongoing IT operations and end-user and technical support.
5. **Application Management** – Application management and enhancements and management of the technical partner program.

6. **Operational Management** – Management of the application developer program and Services Center of Excellence.

Conclusion

CSPS CONTINUE TO SEEK cost-cutting solutions. But at the same time, a CSP now recognizes the need to transform its organizations to serve the emerging converged ICT marketplace. One key step in that process is the ability to bring new services and content to market quickly, and to monetize those services to create new and profitable revenue streams.

Revenue generation is a complex and difficult challenge, and some CSPs have experienced less-than-ideal results when attempting to build siloed solutions. Now, forward-thinking CSPs are addressing this challenge by deploying pre-integrated, hosted Revenue-Generation Engine solutions. The best of those solutions are proven, ready-to-deploy and backed by partners with broad business and technology expertise.

Monetizing data services is key to success in the converged ICT environment; however, success requires a proven revenue-generation approach to avoid the risk of failure.

Endnotes

Forrester. "Surviving in the New U.S. Communications Market," March 2004.

Forrester. "IMS Will Transform Telecom – by 2009," December 2005.

Gartner Dataquest. "Carriers Need New Vision of Next-Generation Service Delivery," August, 2005.

Heavy Reading. "The Future of SDP: Selected Key Findings," November 2005.

Light Reading. "SDP Market Adoption: The Next Wave," September 2005.

Light Reading. "Service Delivery Platforms: The Next Grand Design?," April 2005.

The Moriana Group. "An Operator Guidebook to IMS and Next Generation Networks and Services," August 2005.

The Yankee Group. "Service Delivery Platforms: Moving Toward a Software-Defined Communications Experience," November 2004.

About the Authors

Andreas G. Bauer is the global leader of Communications Industry Frameworks in EDS Portfolio Development. He has over 18 years of experience in business consulting and technology enablement, including careers with IBM Global Services, Deloitte Consulting and Dr. Göhring & Partner Management Consultants. He specializes in marketing and IT strategies, process design and reengineering, IT planning, and management of system implementation projects.

Timothy C. Samler is on the Communications Industry Frameworks team in EDS Portfolio Development. He has over 20 years experience in the communications industry in sales and marketing and IT management including careers with KPMG Management Consulting, Oracle, Nortel Networks and Telus Canada. He is the co-author of the book, *Delighting Customers: How to Win and Retain Loyal Customers.*

The Future Vision of Directory Services

How Technology Is Driving a Revolution in Local Advertising

MAX R. SPEUR

Executive Overview

Today, the Communications Service Provider (CSP) is rethinking its approach to directory services. Some companies have divested directory services entirely. Others have achieved phenomenal success by redefining the very nature of directory services and by finding and exploiting new and profitable sources of advertising revenues. Driven by the growth in online searches, and specifically local online searches, these new directory services will drive online advertising growth over the next half-decade or more.

In this paper, the author examines the influence of technology and new business models on the local advertising business. The paper evaluates the business and service architectures and process models needed to create a more agile, interactive directory- services company and to transform the traditional paper-based business into a new online experience. The author also shows how these strategies are applied in the local advertising marketplace. By changing the ways in which customers find, buy and sell, these new directory services allow consumers to connect anywhere, anytime and any place conveniently.

Beyond the Phone Book

IN THE PAST, WHEN consumers wanted information about products and services, they had just two basic choices: open the phone book or make a call to directory assistance. Those basic directories served well for a generation, and will continue to play a part in the local advertising marketplace.

But today, technology is changing the face of directory services. Consumers now want and will pay for a vast and profitable new range of information, directions and content. Mobile communications, Web-based connectivity and the proliferation of edge devices have opened new and promising channels between buyers and sellers. At the same time, directory-services companies can leverage a new, more-agile directory-services infrastructure to help customers find, experience, buy and acquire a vast array of products, services and content.

Trends in Local Advertising

DRAMATIC CHANGES ARE SWEEPING the local advertising business. Advertiser priorities have shifted significantly, with spending on traditional off-line advertising declining by 5 percent a year, while more interactive on-line advertising is growing by 46 percent annually.[19] Directory-services companies must understand the forces that are reshaping this segment.

---

[19] Australian Financial Review.

Economics

THE FUNDAMENTAL ECONOMICS OF directory services are driving a shift away from traditional print media, including the classic telephone book. As consumers increasingly seek directory information from a growing universe of online sources, and as advertisers shift their spending in pursuit of those customers, traditional print directories face troubling revenue and margin pressures. Because print still represents at least 80 percent of revenues in many markets, directory service providers continue to invest in those traditional businesses. But to prepare for a future that will be dominated by online consumers, more and more CSPs are also planning to invest in online directory-service technologies.

Competition

DUE IN PART TO regulatory protection, competition was virtually non-existent in many directory service markets. But in the emerging world of online searches and directory services, competition is open and global. "Pure" directory service players, like Yahoo! and Google, are forming alliances with local content businesses and with regional television and cable companies, for whom advertising revenue is the primary source of income.

Those pure players are also partnering with new entrants who provide local content for online directory services. Those new entrants typically pursue one of two business models: providing exceptionally low-cost, online content, or leveraging free content to drive Web-based advertising sales.

Value Chain

HISTORICALLY, DIRECTORY SERVICES HAVE relied on a fairly traditional "publishing and manufacturing" value chain. The industry was for decades based on a rather simple and straightforward business model: one centered on printed books such as white pages and yellow pages, driven by space-oriented advertising revenues, and fed in many cases by profit margins of up to 50 percent.

But the emerging Web-based consumer economy is changing the very nature of directory services. As consumers shift their preferences away from hard-copy directories and toward online searches and information, directory services are evolving rapidly toward a value chain driven primarily by "dynamic and interactive content." As a result, most directory services are now highly dynamic and interactive businesses that offer print and online services in parallel.

Challenges to Directory Services

THERE ARE A NUMBER of powerful reasons for companies to pursue a new, converged print and online directory-services model.

First and foremost, consumers are changing the ways in which they work, live and interact. Today's consumers are increasingly mobile. They are connected by a growing array of edge devices, and they are willing to access and use a dazzling universe of new information, communication and entertainment sources. Where consumers go, advertisers will follow; and consumers are increasingly going online for directions, information and communication. By adopting a new print and online-oriented model, a CSP can position itself to benefit from the revenue opportunities of a fully integrated, multi-channel consumer-to-advertiser value chain.

In this new environment, to reach its revenue target, a directory-services company must manage the creation and uptake of new and innovative online products, while also leveraging traditional voice and print products in an integrated way. CSPs can exploit these new models to find and pursue new, high-margin consumer segments and revenue sources. The company can give itself the ability to deliver integrated products and services across networks and channels, thus responding to consumer demand for anytime/anywhere information.

Finally, by simplifying and automating its traditional organization (through a transformation that addresses functions, processes, technology and people), the CSP can create a multi-channel, search-oriented environment that enables consumers and advertisers to benefit from a fully integrated shopping experience.

A New Perspective

TO SUCCEED IN THE coming multi-channel directory-services environment, companies must make a number of fundamental changes.

Most must begin by planning and executing a radical shift away from traditional static and batch process operations—defined by the familiar "sell the ads, produce the book and distribute" cycle—and toward a more dynamic and interactive operating model.

The implication of this shift is that a directory-services business must rethink both its underlying strategic intent and its interaction with clients, both advertisers and consumers. As it alters its most basic strategies, the company faces the mighty task of modernizing its functional organizations, updating its operational business processes, and redefining the role of Information Technology (IT) in its organization.

In the past, IT has played, at best, a supporting role in many directory-services businesses. In the future, as successful companies focus on the acquisition and dissemination of interactive, online content, technology will by necessity become a core element in these businesses. Astute players now view technology as a key enabler, one that allows them to deliver interactive and dynamic directory services across multiple channels, with automated efficiencies and at the lowest possible unit cost.

As part of this paradigm shift, CSPs are now also evaluating a new, partner-based approach to mastering the IT- and technology-driven requirements of this new directory- services marketplace. A typical CSP, having built its directory-services businesses around traditional voice and print products, may not have the technical and support capabilities needed to launch and manage a multi-channel directory-services solution. By partnering with proven IT experts, the CSP can launch next-generation directory services—quickly, cost-effectively and with far less risk.

Of course, a fundamental transformation is not easy. Operational transformation requires hard work, determination, excellent planning and rigorous execution.

Evolving Strategies

WHAT ARE THE STRATEGIES CSPs can employ to compete in the coming directory-services marketplace?

More than in the traditional "find" directory model, the emerging interactive segment will tie a closer link between buyers (consumers) and sellers (advertisers). Directory companies can and should provide research, connections, bookings and transactional services to both buyers and sellers.

In the newer, online-oriented environment, however, CSPs can also benefit by offering a far greater selection of channel access points—including online, voice, wireless and in-car services, in addition to traditional print books. By enhancing the data from the printed books, and by building "need-based" profiles of both advertisers and consumers, a CSP can deliver highly personalized content and services to its subscribers.

A CSP can leverage return on investment tools available in the online environment to provide advertisers with new insights into the created value of its investments. CSPs can use those same capabilities to show advertisers how local content, distributed through other technology platforms, can be used to identify and pursue new vertical consumer categories, thus giving new life to "old" data sources.

Given these changes, directory-services companies are taking a new look at several areas:

Customers

TO COMPETE IN THIS changing marketplace, a directory-services company must work to build strong, integrated and recognized brands within the digital economy. It must leverage its existing brands and channels as differentiators, and position itself to deliver content anywhere, at any time and in any place. Forward-looking CSPs understand the need to attract both traditional off-line, print-based customers and the new and growing universe of online consumers.

To deliver the superior experience demanded by this new generation of consumers, CSPs must bring relevancy to its product portfolios. Often, this translates into the need for a filtered selection of high-quality information directed to individual subscribers, as opposed to the traditional practice of sending an entire book to each and every customer.

Operations

CSPS CAN MEET CONSUMER demand for superior directory services performance by delivering greater usability (through more interactive content and delivery), personalization and contextual awareness. By positioning itself as the consumer's preferred channel for both offline and online directory services, a CSP can attract and hold premium paying advertisers.

This allows the directory business to become a reliable, one-stop merchant for online directions and information. At the same time, the directory service provider can strengthen its traditional core competencies and processes while expanding into new areas of content creation. Thus, a directory publisher can enter the emerging interactive marketplace, while simultaneously differentiating itself from the "pure players" in that segment.

Technology

TRANSFORMING THE TECHNOLOGY INFRASTRUCTURE is critical for directory businesses to enable functions to access, manage, modify, sell and deliver the right content, at the right time, to the right consumer. These new capabilities provide the ability to deliver a quality search response in any place and at any time. It allows a CSP to profile its customers more effectively, while granting managed advertiser access to the end consumer.

Again, these technology changes allow traditional directory businesses to provide a unique quality of content that will set them apart in a crowded and competitive online marketplace.

Transforming Directory Services

ENTERPRISE AGILITY IS A key to companies wanting to compete in the emerging directory- services sector. Organizational agility is the quality that distinguishes companies like Google and Yahoo! from the rest of the pack. To achieve this agility, a CSP must undertake a fundamental transformation in its organization, including key changes in its business model, processes and approach to services. In this context, the desired future state for a successful directory-services firm must address three crucial elements: Business Architecture, an Integrated Process Model and a Service Oriented Architecture (SOA).

Business Architecture

AS SHOWN IN FIGURE 1, an important first step toward creating an agile operating model is to establish an appropriate Business Architecture. This Business Architecture rests on a back-office foundation consisting of network infrastructure and operations support, and a core business platform to manage billing, quality assurance, fulfillment, and business and enterprise management requirements.

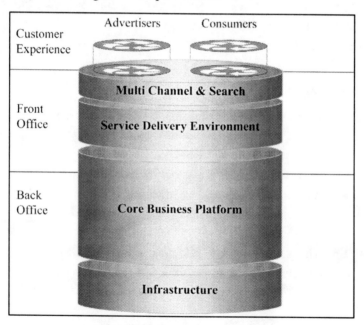

Figure 1 – Business Architecture

Directory Services providers will adopt a more agile, customer-oriented operating model.

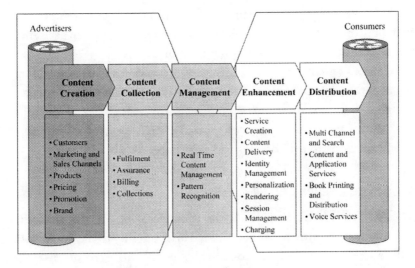

Figure 2 – Integrated Process Model

A content-oriented value chain will define the future of directory services.

The front office layer includes a service delivery environment that handles service creation, transactions and content management, and channel and search capabilities to coordinate identity management and service delivery.

This Business Architecture exists to serve both consumer end-users and advertisers. By pursuing this more agile future vision, directory services can add speed and quality, visibility, reliability and flexibility to their organizations.

Integrated Process Model

DIRECTORY SERVICES CAN BETTER serve both customer groups—consumers and advertisers—by delivering solutions through an Integrated Process Model. As illustrated in Figure 2, this integrated process approach supports a simplified, self-service environment that enables faster, cost-efficient provisioning and activation.

This model addresses content creation. It leverages multiple sales and marketing channels and provides flexibility to manage various products, brands, pricing structures and customer segments. It also supports content collection and management—including storage of structured and unstructured data, real-time content management, pattern recognition and all fulfillment, assurance and billing processes.

Content enhancement includes service creation and delivery, identity management and personalization, rendering, session management and charging. Content distribution can include the logistics of traditional book printing or voice services, plus the management of online and mobile services, multi-channel and search capabilities.

Service Oriented Architecture

A TRUE SOA SUPPORTS the simplification of the underlying technology environment. This approach brings agility to the organization, and can reduce IT-related costs by from 30–50 percent, and those savings can be used to fund additional future investments in interactive directory-services capabilities.

As shown in Figure 3, a SOA consists of a FrontPlane™ containing personalized visualization through portals and reporting mechanisms; a CrossPlane™ that delivers configurable orchestration of data stores and flows, portal integration, and business process and rules engines; a BackPlane™ for enterprise integration; and application components for Customer Relationship Management (CRM), Operations and Enterprise Management.

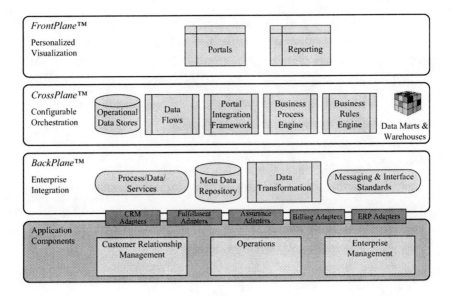

Figure 3 – Service Oriented Architecture

A Service Oriented Architecture supports the delivery of multi-channel directory services.

The SOA allows the creation of a single, holistic view of customers; the proactive management of Service Level Agreements (SLAs) and customer incidents; and the chance to offer cost-efficient self service. This approach also allows directory-services companies to up-sell and cross-sell personalized services based on detailed customer profiles and pattern recognition. Finally, this model supports truly real-time content management and service delivery, effective cost controls, and flexible business analytics and management reports.

The Future of Directory Services Proof Point

WE CAN DEMONSTRATE THE viability of this agility-driven, partnership-based approach by citing the example of a sports-oriented comprehensive portfolio of services that would enable customers to find, buy and sell a variety of golf-related products across multiple channels. This envisioned portfolio included a number of information services, e.g. advertising and online sales, location-based services such as directions to courses and stores, and even access to systems to book tee time. The offering can also include new media and entertainment services, such as golf video delivered via broadcast and Video On Demand (VOD) channels, gaming and customized mobile golf videos.

By building an agile applications and infrastructure environment, this proof point incorporates the following:

- Search capabilities
- One-to-one marketing
- Purchasing, authorization and transaction management
- Location-based services
- Business intelligence
- Revenue and transaction reporting

Advertising

DIRECTORY-SERVICES ADVERTISING WILL BE enhanced with online functionality, including service access and identity management, charging, service control with process workflow and subscriber management. This will allow the golf vertical to generate incremental revenues, track customer behavior and improve the overall customer experience.

Online Shopping

THIS PROPOSAL WILL ALLOW golf consumers to purchase online, where the CSP provides a secure data environment. This online shopping environment will give a CSP an easy-to-use, cost-efficient, self-service shopping and location-based service that drive new revenues and customer loyalty.

Monetizing Services

THIS MORE AGILE, INTERACTIVE approach to directory services will allow the company to offer an expanded service catalog, and to accept, host, manage and deliver a vastly expanded range of golf-related content. The company can leverage the agile platform to open new revenue streams—from selling rich media content, to offering a more complete and satisfying experience to its customers, and to expanding its overall market scope and reach significantly.

Conclusion

THE NATURE AND POTENTIAL of directory services is changing. Consumers once had a limited number of choices when they needed to find and buy products and services. But technology and new business models are radically altering the face of local advertising.

Today's consumers can access content and products through a dazzling array of devices, mobile services and on-line sources. CSPs are seeing a steady decline in revenues from traditional print books and voice directory services. At the same time, revenues from interactive, multi-channel advertising, content and products continue to grow.

While a few large new players dominate online advertising, traditional directory-services companies can compete and win in this evolving space. By adopting a strategy that embraces new methods and channels of delivery, and by partnering with an IT provider to attain the infrastructure and support needed to operationalize those capabilities, directory service companies can succeed in this growing market segment.

About the Author

Max R. Speur has had significant international experience in the communications industry in Europe and Asia Pacific. He is currently the Asia Pacific communications industry leader for EDS. In this role, Speur is responsible for innovation, thought leadership and demand creation, and for enabling clients' growth. Speur was with IBM Global Services previously, where he served as business development executive on a variety of engagements in Thailand, China, India and Australia.

A Collaborative ICT Approach

Go-to-Market Strategies in the Converged ICT Space

ALBERTO BALESTRAZZI
ANDREAS G. BAUER
PAUL M. MORRISON

Executive Overview

We have seen how the communications industry has evolved. The communications and Information Technology (IT) industries are rapidly converging. Communications Service Providers (CSPs) now see a very real opportunity to deliver increasingly data-driven, business-oriented solutions in this emerging market. But those IT-centric services require new and complex capabilities. By forging collaborative partnerships with proven IT outsourcing specialists, CSPs can more fully exploit the potential of the converged Information and Communications Technology (ICT) market.

The authors describe the obstacles CSPs face in this converged market, and they demonstrate how CSPs can collaborate with the right partners to develop and execute go-to-market strategies and take product and services to market more quickly and efficiently. They attempt to show how product road maps, sales channels and delivery capabilities can be aligned to create a successful partner ecosystem for the ICT marketplace.

Convergence Is Here

THE COMMUNICATIONS INDUSTRY HAS reached the crossroad of service convergence, and this change is evident along several dimensions.

Wireline and wireless services are converging. Some incumbent CSPs, for example, want to offer converged wireless, Voice over Internet Protocol (VoIP) services to compete against pure wireless players.

Voice, video and data services are converging into the "triple play" of communications. Other CSPs are now offering Internet Protocol Television (IPTV) services to compete against cable operators and Multiple Service Operators (MSOs) that are now pushing voice services into the communications market place.

At the same time, communications and IT services are converging, with CSPs now looking for the business and technical resources needed to sell, deliver and support a wide range of data-oriented solutions.

CSPs understand that to survive and succeed in this converged marketplace, content and applications services must be integrated across network technologies. More importantly, those services, and the go-to-market strategies that are required to drive any communications business, must be adapted to the needs and expectations of each specific customer segment.

Communications and IT Convergence

CSPS, WHICH HAVE TRADITIONALLY provided access, connectivity and managed network services, are now exploring ways to offer an entirely new range of service bundles. Those potential new services range from desktop support to hosting, managed services, content management, systems integration, consulting, business process management and outsourcing.

But while CSPs are working to refine and launch data services, this marketplace poses significant hurdles for companies that have long focused primarily on access and connectivity. A CSP must consider the complexity of IT-centric solutions. They must consider its operational requirements—what it takes to sell and deliver those solutions, and the cost of penetrating and serving those data-centric markets.

To tackle the IT segment, most CSPs will need to make substantial investments to build the service capabilities required to launch and support data-oriented services. Those investments are needed at a time when many CSPs still struggle to maintain value from legacy network systems.

Except for the large tier 1 players, few CSPs enjoy the economies of scale needed to compete efficiently in the already-crowded, IT-services marketplace. Most CSPs struggle to attain the sales capabilities needed to compete in this market space. Few have the global reach needed to penetrate and serve multinationals across the globe.

CSPs are striving to overcome these inherent limitations, often by internally building or buying IT capabilities. Some have worked with Systems Integrators (SIs) and outsourcers; however, without a proven go-to-market strategy, most have not succeeded in delivering value-added solutions to the business marketplace. In attempting to arrange value-chain strategies, CSPs have struggled with the issues of balance and control, the ability to satisfy all service and delivery requirements and the equitable division of responsibility and value.

CSPs must also manage customer service in the more complex, data-oriented end of the spectrum. The customer experience must be seamless, from the initial order through service delivery and support. The introduction of data services carries a high execution risk and will require most CSPs to revise, or at least to enhance a number of key skill sets, including sales, billing, customer support and partner relations.

From an IT standpoint, legacy fulfillment, assurance and billing IT systems must be replaced or upgraded to handle new data requirements.

A CSP must manage seamless and cost-efficient integration and interoperability between its existing infrastructure and the new data-centric, IP-based networks. Most must master the new and difficult complexities of content ingestion and storage, revenue assurance and digital rights management.

What's more, all of these changes must take place while the CSP continues to manage existing networks and services in a competitive market environment.

Addressing the Market Segments

TODAY, A GROWING NUMBER of CSPs understand the importance of forging a collaborative alliance with an IT partner in order to deliver value-added solutions in this converged marketplace—particularly to serve customers in the most complex enterprise market segment. There is growing awareness that an IT partner with proven experience in selling, delivering and supporting data services is vital to a CSPs success.

While CSPs recognize and pursue a range of micro-segments, most potential customers fall within three primary groupings. To understand the promise and challenge of these segments in the converged ICT space, it is useful to examine each in some detail.

Enterprise

THE ENTERPRISE MARKET IS defined by the convergence of fixed and mobile services, a high degree of custom integration, and the need to manage IT and networking infrastructure of multinational corporations that require global support. Enterprise services typically require complex provisioning, assurance and billing to support a broad product portfolio serving a diverse set of user requirements. Most CSPs struggle to obtain IT credibility in this part of the enterprise space.

To serve the enterprise market together with IT players, companies must adopt a contracting model that is changing from the traditional model of "selling services through IT vendors" to a model of "selling with vendors." This requires a shift to a more cooperative, alliance-based selling model.

Companies that hope to succeed in the enterprise space must develop new channels, customer relationships, brand positioning and delivery capabilities. This typically requires a significant investment—spending that few but the largest CSPs can afford or justify at this time.

Small Office/Home Office, Small and Medium-Sized Enterprises

CSPS ARE PURSUING THE Small Office/Home Office (SOHO) and Small, Medium Enterprise (SME) marketplace with mixed success. This space is defined by the need for bundled communications services, a lower level of customization than the enterprise segment, and a higher price sensitivity. These enterprises want business-quality voice and messaging services, mobile applications, and seamless access for mobile phones, Personal Digital Assistants (PDAs), laptops and other devices. To serve these businesses, service providers must deliver a limited number of business services at consumer-level prices. They must leverage economies of scale, both from the consumer-oriented telecom side and from the business-oriented side of the IT outsourcer.

Consumer

CONSUMERS WANT COMMUNICATIONS THAT are fun, personalized and that deliver fast and convenient access to a growing universe of media and content. To deliver a seamless consumer experience—including after-sales support and a competent help-desk experience—companies also need IT partnerships that help reduce the cost of service delivery. CSPs have traditionally served the consumer marketplace well, but as subscribers demand increasingly data-oriented services and applications, service providers must gain new IT-oriented sales, product and support capabilities.

A Partnering Approach

TO PENETRATE AND SERVE these segments successfully, CSPs must acquire a new and far broader set of competences. But market experience has shown that few communications companies can successfully address this convergent market alone. Looking forward, CSPs are now collaborating with a select class of IT players to approach and serve the ICT marketplace. Those uniquely qualified IT players are working with service providers to identify and open new sources of revenue in this converged environment, along the entire value chain, from product development to sales to service (see Figure 1).

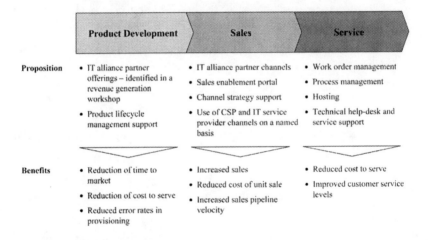

Product Development	Sales	Service
Proposition		
• IT alliance partner offerings – identified in a revenue generation workshop	• IT alliance partner channels	• Work order management
	• Sales enablement portal	• Process management
	• Channel strategy support	• Hosting
• Product lifecycle management support	• Use of CSP and IT service provider channels on a named basis	• Technical help-desk and service support
Benefits		
• Reduction of time to market	• Increased sales	• Reduced cost to serve
• Reduction of cost to serve	• Reduced cost of unit sale	• Improved customer service levels
• Reduced error rates in provisioning	• Increased sales pipeline velocity	

Figure 1 – IT Service Providers and Alliance Partners
Working with CSPs: Proposition and Benefits

Because they understand and serve the data-oriented segments, IT players can open new opportunities by improving the efficiency of CSP operations, by developing and managing sales cycles, by improving customer service and by implementing and operating the front- and back-office technology platforms needed to compete in this market.

To establish or expand its position in the data services market, a CSP needs to seek IT partners that offer a distinct and proven set of capabilities. An ideal IT partner will offer the following:

- A proven and substantial investment in data service capabilities

- A flexible, low-risk infrastructure and the global reach needed to drive cost reduction and growth
- A market-proven road map for product marketing, delivery and support
- A broad alliance ecosystem that addresses key marketing, product solution, IT and systems integration needs
- Complementary operational capabilities, with the technical and process expertise to deliver comprehensive ICT solutions to business markets
- Proven revenue-generation models
- Service Delivery Platforms (SDPs) built on industry-standard architectures and adaptable to serve any segment of the converged marketplace
- A track record of meeting enterprise-class Service Level Agreements (SLAs)
- An established and proven sales capability in the IT services marketplace
- IT service assets and expertise to drive innovation in the data services sector

By combining their respective strengths and capabilities, both the CSP and the IT service provider can benefit from this collaborative relationship.

They can create integrated solutions together that operate seamlessly across networks and market segments. These cooperative partners can build and operate the support infrastructure needed to deliver new services and to reduce time-to-market. They can leverage efficiencies and economies of scale to drive down costs and meet demanding service-level expectations.

By exploiting traditional market positions, a data-oriented IT provider and an access-oriented CSP can target and serve customers across the converged marketplace spectrum. These collaborative partners can then leverage each other's brands, and the brands of top business and technical alliance partners, adding measurable value and enhancing the customer perception of the combined offering.

The Collaborative Methodology

TO SUCCEED, A COLLABORATIVE revenue-generation approach to the ICT marketplace must be driven by a proven methodology. That approach must address product development, sales and marketing, service delivery and support.

A good collaborative approach begins with a clear definition of the proposed partnership. The CSP, IT service provider and its alliance partners must evaluate and agree upon an important set of alliance elements. Those elements can include the product/services road map, business case, market and channel strategies, partner capabilities, roles, responsibilities and the equitable division of value.

These issues are best addressed in a series of formal marketing and engagement workshops attended by all key partnership members (see Figure 2). Marketing-oriented workshops allow CSPs and partners to evaluate which products should be brought to market and the implications of those offerings on sales channels, business processes, applications and IT infrastructure.

Customer Marketing Workshops

Engagement Workshops

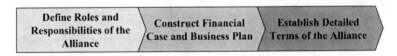

Figure 2 – Customer Marketing and Engagement Workshops

By focusing initially on a few select solutions, alliance partners can determine the capabilities needed to deliver those solutions across the value chain. These early evaluations should focus on the existing resources and capabilities of the consortium parties, and the business terms, roles and responsibilities and financial flows needed to launch, deliver and profit from the offerings.

The CSP and IT service provider should finalize a formal document of understanding to define this crucial business and technical relationship. Once established, this basic operational model—defining routes to market, roles and financial benefits—will serve to guide the alliance as it pursues new and expanded opportunities in the converged ICT marketplace.

Conclusion

CONVERGENCE IS A REALITY in the communications and IT industries—a trend that is reshaping the products, channels, technologies and players in the marketplace. CSPs can now realistically hope to serve customers in all segments of this converged marketplace, from delivering traditional voice services to providing bundled, data-oriented solutions to consumers, small and medium-sized enterprises and corporate businesses.

But to compete in the more complex ICT environment, CSPs need a new and far broader set of market and technology competences. Few service providers have the size or resources to tackle those challenges on their own. Fewer still can afford to buy their way into this space. A new collaborative go-to-market model can address the marketing, product, infrastructure and support requirements of the converged marketplace. By forging alliances with a leading IT service provider, as well as other well selected business and technology partners, CSPs can quickly and economically target, penetrate and serve data-oriented segments.

Endnotes

Gartner Group Focus Report. "IT Services: Identifying the Addressable Markets for Telecom Operators," 2005.

Gartner Group Research Brief. "Carriers Collide With IT Services Providers," 2003.

Gartner Group, Strategic Planning, SPA-21-8970. "Global Telecom Outsourcers Need New Skills to Win Big Firms."

Stratecast Partners Insights for Executives (SPIE #20). "Outsourcing Relationships Integral to 'Service Providers' Enterprise Success."

Technology Business Research. "Telecom Infrastructure Services," 2004.

About the Authors

Alberto Balestrazzi is a client industry executive at EDS for major telecom accounts in Europe, Middle East and Africa (EMEA). He is responsible for innovation, thought leadership and demand creation, and for enabling growth and transformation for clients. He brings more than 18 years of experience in the communications industry. He has worked as a management and technology consultant for major operators across Europe. Balestrazzi has held leadership roles with IBM, A.T. Kearney, Booz Allen Hamilton and Accenture.

Andreas G. Bauer is the global leader of Communications Industry Frameworks in EDS Portfolio Development. He has over 18 years of experience in business consulting and technology enablement, including careers with IBM Global Services, Deloitte Consulting and Dr. Göhring & Partner Management Consultants. He specializes in marketing and IT strategies, process design and reengineering, IT planning, and management of system implementation projects.

Paul M. Morrison is a client industry executive in the EDS Global Communications Industry Group. He has more than 20 years of experience in management and information technology, supporting telecommunications clients in the Americas, Europe, Middle East, Africa and Asia that are in the midst of significant change. Previously, he was a partner and executive at IBM Global Services and also had careers at A.T. Kearney, McKinsey and BP.

New Models of Collaboration in the ICT Market

How Communications Service Providers and IT Service Firms Can Create a Balanced Shared-Value Approach to the ICT Marketplace

SEBASTIÃO M. BURIN
RENATO OSATO

Executive Overview

Communications Service Providers (CSPs) now face a market characterized by falling Average Revenue per User (ARPU), shifting revenue sources and increasingly converged global communications. Forward-looking CSPs now see data-oriented services as the key to new growth and profitability. But to support those more complex applications, and to serve the challenging corporate Small, Medium Enterprise (SME) and consumer segments, telecommunications companies need far more robust and responsive Information Technology (IT) service capabilities.

Today, a growing number of CSPs are adopting a collaborative alliance approach to respond to the challenges of delivering IT-centric support.

In this paper, the authors examine the requirements of delivering Information Services (IS) in an increasingly IT-driven communications marketplace. They evaluate the models now used to deliver IS, and discuss a collaborative strategy in which CSPs and IT service providers create a balanced, shared-value approach to the Information and Communications Technology (ICT) marketplace.

The Changing Telecommunications Market

CSPS MUST ADAPT TO a rapidly changing marketplace.

Mobile communications continue to grow on a global basis. At the same time, Voice over IP (VoIP) continues to cannibalize traditional sources of CSP revenue. The worldwide telecommunications market is growing, but as providers face new competition and enter lower-income markets, they must adapt to declining rates of ARPU.

Broadband is gaining acceptance, but not at a pace sufficient to offset continued losses in most fixed-line business for most CSPs. Newer technologies can open untapped markets and segments, but they typically require significant investments at the point-of-presence and in handsets. Additionally, these new markets and segments attract new players and competitors.

It is not surprising, then, that astute CSPs are seeking new markets and new strategies to penetrate, serve and profit from those emerging segments.

Segment Demands

IN THIS ENVIRONMENT, PERHAPS the most promising opportunities for CSPs lay in delivering a broader spectrum of solutions and new value-added services to corporate, SME and consumer customers. Consumers are responding to a wide range of content-heavy information, entertainment and personalization services, and a smart provider is getting in position to serve this data-driven marketplace.

Consumers are responding to a wide range of content-heavy information, entertainment and personalization services, and a smart provider is getting in position to serve this data-driven marketplace. SMEs now want business-class communications and messaging services, mobile solutions and seamless access to their enterprise systems, in addition to managed IT infrastructure and business application services. Some CSPs pursue the more complex and demanding corporate segment, which can be served by offerings that include converged fixed and mobile solutions, VoIP, and customized enterprise applications.

CSP Challenges

CSPS HAVE ENCOUNTERED A number of challenges when striving to serve these market segments.

Many telcos have found it very difficult to deal with the smaller content and application vendors that support these segments. Those smaller firms are often undercapitalized and can rarely meet the Service Level Agreement (SLA) requirements of CSP end customers. CSPs can also find it difficult to process and manage content from a myriad of sources and to coordinate revenue assurance and digital-rights management.

To deliver the services required to sell and support IT-based applications, a typical CSP must invest heavily to acquire or re-skill both its support staff and its direct and indirect sales channels. Each of the many segments in the data-oriented marketplace requires specialized and difficult-to-reuse technical support. At the same time, business process services, such as field services and contact center operations, have become commoditized, driving down margins and requiring very large-scale operations to be profitable.

By the same token, many IT services, like hosting or workplace management, require multi-customer, low-cost, global delivery capabilities—but still provide relatively low margins.

Existing fulfillment, billing and IT systems typically cannot handle the requirements of data-centric applications and services. In fact, those legacy systems can often impede the adoption of more helpful and cost-effective, self-service solutions. Vertically oriented customer service systems make it hard to handle multi-service customer inquiries or to maximize cross selling opportunities. When CSPs move to an Internet Protocol (IP)-based, data-centric network environment, existing infrastructure must be managed to retirement in an efficient and cost-effective way that requires a considerable amount of management talent and attention.

Unlike support for traditional voice services, support for IT-based services is a more complex and dynamic challenge, requiring close monitoring and fast responses to prevent costly problems. In many cases, current infrastructures reduce the CSP's agility and can limit its ability to grow, launch new services and create innovative partnerships.

Finally, it is inherently risky for a CSP to make all of the needed changes in skill sets, internal systems, sales, billing, customer support and partner relations. A failure in any one of these crucial areas can reduce efficiencies, harm customer satisfaction and delay or reduce revenue flows.

Collaborative Models

THAT IS WHY CSPS are increasingly seeking new and more effective ways to service and support the data-oriented needs of the ICT marketplace. Several new service models have now emerged to meet those needs, and CSPs should carefully consider the advantages and disadvantages of these available strategies.

The Integrated Model

IN THE INTEGRATED APPROACH, the telco's internal IS organization provides services to both internal IS users as well as to external clients. To handle the scale and complexity of the services required to support its markets and applications, a CSP calls on outsourcing providers for key IT services.

Under the Integrated approach, a CSP can leverage the scale, infrastructure and capabilities of both its own IS organization and the outsourcing services provider. But this model also creates intrinsic conflicts between the needs of internal and external IS clients, and can hinder Profit & Loss (P&L) transparency in the CSP organization.

The Independent Model

UNDER THE INDEPENDENT MODEL, a CSP creates and owns an independent, market-facing organization to provide IS to both internal CSP users and to external clients. Some CSPs leverage the Independent approach to penetrate the ICT marketplace aggressively.

But this Independent approach also suffers from several key limitations. Because the telecommunications operator now competes in the outsourcing space, it looses the opportunity to partner with other outsourcing providers that can offer exceptional scale, capabilities and market reach. Because the outsourcing company belongs to the telco group, it may limit competition for many CSP IT service contracts.

A Specialized Model

THE SPECIALIZED APPROACH LEVERAGES an independent organization to deliver IS to external clients. This specialized market-facing organization might be a division or business unit of the CSP, and is created specifically to deliver IS to external clients. A traditional internal IS organization provides similar service to internal telco departments.

Within the Specialized model, many CSPs also call on the services of an allied outsourcer to support both the market-facing organization and the internal IS group.

The Specialized model allows CSPs to achieve true P&L transparency and a consistent business model with minimum conflict between internal and external clients. This Specialized approach enables the telco to leverage resources available from an allied outsourcer to more precisely meet the specific demands of external market segments.

Partnering Considerations

IN ANY MODEL, THE key is to find the most appropriate approach to have the required skills and experience (meaning delivery capability) to go to market. Some CSPs considered acquiring those capabilities or building them internally. But the time and cost needed to acquire such capabilities led many CSPs to consider a new direction.

CSPs now recognize the value of a more cooperative, alliance-based approach to delivering IS. To succeed, a collaborative partnership must provide clear and measurable benefits to both the CSP and the outsourcing service provider.

A truly workable go-to-market strategy should be balanced, transparent and focused on the creation and sharing of mutual value. The best collaborations seek to identify and optimize economies of scale, while reducing churn and enhancing end-user satisfaction and loyalty. Thus, an ideal CSP/outsourcer partnership searches for fair and equitable ways to share both the workload and the value chain.

Let's examine some of the specific requirements of a successful CSP/IS provider collaboration.

Seeking Mutual Value

A CSP CAN MAXIMIZE its opportunities in these emerging data-centric market segments by forming positive collaborations with carefully selected Systems Integrators (SIs) and outsourcing service providers.

In the enterprise marketplace, CSPs can partner with qualified outsourcers to create and market portfolios that add value for all participants. This arrangement can typically succeed by evolving from a sell-though contracting model toward a more balanced sell-with approach. On a more limited scale, both partners can also create jointly customized solutions for clients.

In the SME sector, telcos can partner to acquire the IT capabilities needed to handle complex service management challenges. To succeed in the SME segments, collaborative alliances should focus on strengthening product portfolios and delivery capabilities and on enabling channels to sell and deliver services at a competitive price.

The Small Office/Home Office (SOHO) segment is traditionally very price sensitive. CSPs should seek partnerships that deliver economies of scale capable of providing business-class services at consumer prices. To reach and serve the consumer market, CSPs must collaborate with partners that can reduce the cost of service with a consistent delivery model that spans various product lines.

The benefits for the CSP and the outsourcer are closely related to the new addressable market available to them.

Building Complementary Capabilities

IN THE ICT SPACE, a well-suited IT partner can naturally complement the product development capabilities of the CSP.

Hardware and software vendors, for example, can assist market strategy and product design efforts, including customer segmentation and competitive analysis, portfolio management and product conceptualization. Those same hardware and software suppliers can also support product marketing and offer management and elements of sales and distribution.

IT services companies, on the other hand, can provide important product-oriented technical input, application development and integration services and various other service elements. IT service firms can also assist with IT infrastructure operations, including service integration and testing, service delivery, hosting and provisioning, application management, the management of SLAs, field services and help desk and trouble management. A reliable IT partner can also provide important customer care operations, like product and technical end-user support.

The actual division of work will, of course, depend on the existing capabilities and market needs of the participants in each alliance. By calling on a trusted IT firm to handle these crucial activities, the CSP can concentrate on business planning, content creation and acquisition, sales and lead generation, network management and other core functions.

The Approach to Collaboration

WE PROPOSE A BALANCED, cooperative strategy that allows CSPs and IT service providers to share both the workload and the value of delivering support in these ICT market segments.

This approach is based on the fact that, in reality, there is a relatively small potential market conflict between most CSPs and the IT outsourcer. As a proven IT solutions provider, the IT outsourcer most naturally serves a market consisting primarily of regional and global corporations and large local companies.

Most CSPs focus primarily on SME, SOHO and consumer market segments, as well as government entities, addressing some local, regional and global corporations. CSPs typically pursue tens of thousands of business clients, while the IT outsourcer is focused heavily on a list of hundreds of clients and prospects. Often, the IT outsourcer does not maintain an indirect sales channel that could conflict with most CSP indirect sales channels.

By forging a balanced collaborative alliance, CSPs and IT service providers can continue to pursue their distinct natural markets, while at the same time pursuing a large and profitable joint addressable market segment.

As illustrated in Figure 1, this joint approach allows the CSP to maintain its traditional direct and Value Added Reseller (VAR) market channels, while leveraging outsourced IT service capabilities to realize higher revenues, greater profitability and new market opportunities.

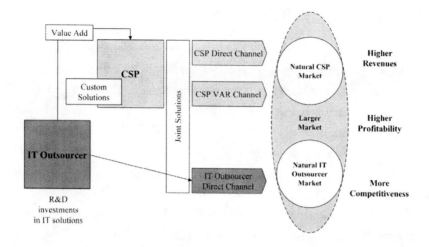

Figure 1 – The Advantages of a Joint Addressable Marketplace

CSPs can also benefit from the creation of a joint value-added portfolio. When added to the telco's traditional investment in communications, the additional capabilities delivered by the IT service provider can bring differentiation and value to the CSPs product mix. These complementary solutions can include a wide range of infrastructure technology outsourcing services, such as managed data center services, data optimization and storage, enterprise-class security and workplace management. The services offered do not necessarily need to be joint solutions; the CSP can also offer some of the IT outsourcer's portfolio directly, if these services can be used by the CSP's clients without modifications.

Other IT support services can include application development and management, and business process outsourcing for help desks, contact centers or transaction processing.

This approach also allows a CSP to leverage the global alliance relationships of an IT outsourcer. Such federations of market-leading companies—which could include network equipment providers and hardware and software vendors—are a core benefit of the collaborative philosophy. The alliance relationships can provide proven multi-vendor IT services delivery solutions, access to world-class innovation and an established value added ICT portfolio.

Benefits of Collaboration

A COLLABORATIVE ALLIANCE CAN yield significant benefits for both the CSP and the IT outsourcing provider.

By establishing a joint go-to-market initiative, CSPs and IT service providers can leverage the power of existing alliances, combine existing investments, and magnify the market power of each partner's facilities, assets and capabilities.

When supported by a qualified IT outsourcer, a CSP can leverage that partner's existing investment in data-oriented systems, infrastructure and expertise. For example, an experienced IT firm will have an operating service delivery architecture and business managements systems that are designed specifically to support today's emerging class of IP-oriented managed services.

A well-conceived alliance can help improve SLA performance, reduce costs and capital requirements and open new marketing opportunities. CSPs can leverage a well-planned alliance to reduce time to market and to flatten the learning curve needed to penetrate and exploit data-driven market segments.

Conclusion

CSPS FACE THE REALITY of changing market demand, tighter margins and more competitive global realities. As fixed-line revenues flatten or decline, many telcos now see providing data-oriented services to consumer and business markets as an important source of future growth and revenue.

But a CSP also realizes it must make important changes to serve this emerging data-driven communications marketplace. Current-generation sales, back office, customer service systems simply cannot meet the technical and support requirements of the ICT segments. Operators require new and more robust IT solutions capable of meeting the demands of converged services, in order to reduce churn and open new revenue opportunities.

While some CSPs have attempted to build internal support infrastructures, most have found those efforts to be costly and less-than-effective. Increasingly, CSPs are seeking a more efficient collaborative approach that leverages the proven capabilities of experienced IT service providers. Leveraging this collaborative model, CSPs are forging balanced and mutually beneficial alliances in which support functions, responsibilities and the value chain are shared in a logical and equitable way.

As proven in a growing number of real-world situations, the cooperative approach advocated in this paper can deliver measurable market and financial benefits for both the CSP and the IT service provider.

About the Authors

Sebastião M. Burin is a client executive for the Communications Industry in EDS Latin America. He is responsible for building and sustaining strong relationships with clients and for developing new business opportunities for EDS. Burin's experience spans over 20 years in the IT industry, including a career with Booz Allen Hamilton. He has significant experience in systems development and consulting for a variety of industries, especially telecommunications and financial services. Burin specializes in IT strategy and IT transformation, from definition through implementation.

Renato Osato is a client industry executive for the Communications Industry in Latin America. He is responsible for innovation, thought leadership, demand creation, and for enabling growth and transformation for clients. He has over 17 years of professional experience in IT, with previous careers at Unisys, Telemar and Accenture. He served a number of communications clients around Latin America, including fixed-line carriers, cellular companies and pay-TV operators. Osato specializes in IT planning and systems integration implementation.

Part IV:

Future Outlook

WE BELIEVE THAT CSPS must operate in an agile environment to compete in an increasingly digital world. This final section covers our view of the digital world and how CSPs can capture future business opportunities.

The Agile Telecommunications Customer

What Is the Impact of the Digital Lifestyle on Telecommunications Providers?

RENÉ J. AERDTS, PH.D.

Executive Overview

The mantra, "If we build it, they will come," is no longer true in today's fast-changing society. Yesterday's world of vendor- and product-driven marketing has been replaced by consumer- and service-driven demand. As a result of this shift, the focus of the telecommunications industry is that of a telecommunications-driven digital ecosystem in support of the consumer-driven digital lifestyle.

The interaction between this ecosystem and the consumer lifestyle creates new business opportunities for Communications Service Providers (CSPs). At the same time, CSPs need to understand the customer's view in this fluid ecosystem. These customers are known as "agile telecommunications customers," as they want to leverage the components they already have, while enabling new functionality at an ever faster speed. This increasing demand for change requires that a CSP prepare itself for constant change.

In this paper, the author describes the digital lifestyle, the impact on businesses, consumers and the CSP and the transformational changes that must take place in the industry to support this lifestyle.

The Digital Lifestyle

THE DIGITAL LIFESTYLE IS really an extension of digitizing that has taken place in the business world and in our personal lives. It started off with digitizing corporate assets and resources (with the promise of a paperless office, which has yet to materialize). The journey continued with digitizing personal assets, which have become more accessible and more affordable as technology has advanced.

Now we find ourselves in the initial stages of the next phase of digitization in the personal environment: digitization around the "things" (or devices) that we use to communicate with other people or "things." In the past, the focus was on hardware and software. As a result, transactions and data were originated with human intervention, with interactions focused on people-to-people, people-to-things, and things-to-people (see Figure 1).

With the "edge" defined as the point where data and transactions originate, in an edge computing era, the majority of interactions will occur between things: the things-to-things interaction will obliterate the three other types of interactions from the pre-edge computing era (see Figure 1). This type of interaction requires the digitization of all interactions and data associated with the interaction. Welcome to the digital lifestyle!

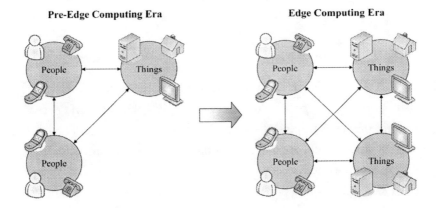

Figure 1 – Transformation into Edge Computing Era

As the interaction between devices becomes more prevalent, it is important to realize that services will become mainstream, and even a requirement. Without services, personal interaction and intervention will still be needed. In a world where time is becoming a scarce resource, services will enable the device-to-device interaction to allow users to focus on those things that are important: making decision based on the data and information provided by the devices.

As an example, it is anticipated that in the year 2012, there will be more than a trillion Radio Frequency Identifiers (RFIDs). All these RFIDs are of limited use unless they can communicate with each other and with corporate systems to enable supply chain integration and optimization. This is a prime example of "things" communicating with other "things" and systems.

Customers vs. Vendors and Markets

WITH THE ADVENT OF the Internet, consumers gained access to an abundance of information, and through this access, the consumer became more empowered. This change is leading consumers to select, and in some instances demand services in a much more informed way, much as corporations have done. These requests are transforming the market from a vendor- and product-oriented towards a service-oriented model.

The Apathetic Customer

SIMPLICITY IS KEY IN today's consumer-centric environment. The consumer markets for telecommunications, personal video and personal audio are prime examples of this trend. Whereas integrated consumer products have market appeal, the simplest designs and functionality are found in single-function devices, such as the personal Digital Versatile Disc (DVD) player and personal audio players. As technology matures, other functions and features are integrated. A manifestation of this trend is the MP3 player, which started as a single function device (to play songs), and evolved to integrate a video capability. As technology advances, streaming video will be a natural progression.

The major overriding trend is the fact that this progression of functionality is based on simplicity of design and use. At the same time, the functions are no longer provided only by the device manufacturers. Consumers increasingly provide input on the functions and features that are needed, with market research responding to these requests with the appropriate development and pricing strategies. For example, see how Instant Messaging (IM) has evolved. It was available on the computer at first, but as consumers became more mobile, CSPs started to offer it on phones to meet consumer demand.

Resistance to Change

ONE OF THE KEY inhibitors to the introduction and acceptance of new devices and services is the natural resistance to change. In the past, the saying was: "If it is not broken, don't fix it." In the current world, where change is occurring at an ever-increasing pace, this saying has changed to "If it is not broken, break it."

This subtle change has a tremendous impact to both the personal and business environments. The majority of consumers tend to stick with technologies with which they are familiar, and they adopt upgrades when available. Most consumers accept incremental changes, whereas early adopters embrace new products and services. The resistance by most consumers to abrupt change allows companies and CSPs to introduce new products and services as a pace that fits their business model.

Convergence is now also a reality; in fact, it is occurring between voice and data as well as the fixed and mobile. CSPs are expected to offer integrated consumer-oriented products and services seamlessly across their networks. As shown in Figure 2, the customer experience should consist of a single integrated interface, which is customizable based on the role of the consumer at that time. This common interface allows CSPs to support the proliferation of edge devices, and to leverage the "building block" product approach that makes them more agile: faster speed-to-market, less overlap and tighter integration.

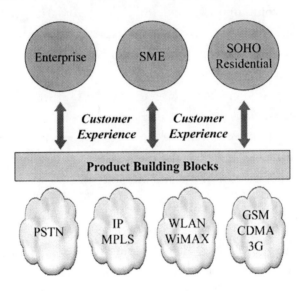

Figure 2 – Convergence at Many Levels

The Generational Effect

AS WE HAVE SEEN above, businesses and consumers are starting to drive the changes in the connected world. In the past, most of the momentum for change was driven by the economic possibilities of the consumer. Even though this is still a very important factor, the market force and sheer number of people requiring a function or feature is becoming more important. This change implies that we must examine not only the available spend, but also current and future demographics.

Even though we need to focus on the new generation of workers, we also need to pay attention to the aging workforce. According to the U.S. Department of Labor[20] report, in 2010, more than 50 percent of the workforce will be 40 or older; whereas the percentage of workers in the age group between 16–24 is steadily declining. The next-generation workforce (the teenagers and pre-teenagers) has six distinctive characteristics. They are: independent, individualistic, informed, instantaneous, interactive and invisible.

The current generation of teens is attuned to an always-on voice, video and data communications network. The boundaries between these different types of access mechanism are blurred, or even non-existent, for this generation, whereas those boundaries still exist for the older generations.

The agile customer that is targeted by the CSPs needs to include these two opposite sides of the spectrum: the young generation that is quick to adopt (and even demand) new technology, new features and additional functions, as well as the more mature generation looking for robust functionality, ease of use and integration.

The Fashion Thing

IN THE PAST, CONSUMER telecommunications equipment was viewed and positioned as a necessity, with the functionality driving the form factor of the device. These days, with the younger generation driving much of the explosive growth and use of these devices and associated services, devices have become a fashion accessory. In fact, this shift moved the device from a functionality-driven to a fashion-driven appliance.

Current telecommunication devices not only come in different colors, sizes and form factors, but also incorporate other personal infotainment features, such as the MP3 player. Through this convergence, CSPs open

---

[20] U.S. Department of Labor, Bureau of Labor Statistics. The US Economy to 2010, 2001.

up new revenue streams, especially when they forge relationships with non-traditional telecommunications providers such as music, video and content providers.

Real and Perceived Security

MOBILE COMMUNICATION IS NOW where the Internet was four or five years ago—particularly in relation to mobile commerce (m-commerce). In this realm, security is needed to protect the interest of the consumers and commerce partners. This security should be built-in, simple, and "always on." In other words, security should be entirely transparent to the end user.

These security features must incorporate both physical and logical security. As devices become smaller and contain more and more personal and business information, it is critical that the physical asset is protected. At the same time, unauthorized use of these assets should be prevented, as more corporate information becomes accessible through these devices. With consumers storing more personal information in the digital format, they want that data protected in case the devices are misplaced, stolen or damaged.

It Is All Too Difficult

NEW TECHNOLOGIES USUALLY INCLUDE new interfaces. As outlined above, the acceptance of these newer types of technologies may be delayed because of resistance to change or acceptance of the new technology, or fear of the impact these technologies might have on business and personal lives.

Simplification is key to the acceptance of any new or changed technologies. A gradual transition from old to new, or a seamless integration of new and older technology, becomes key to acceptance, especially with the older generation of consumers.

The Application of Applications

THE MANTRA "INFORMATION IS king" is not dead at all. In fact, in today's information-rich society, we could update it to read: "Content is king." And content is exactly what CSPs are focusing on delivering.

In the telecommunications world (and especially in the wireless area), the ongoing search is for the "killer application." However, as it turns out, consumers focus more on the content than on applications. This fine distinction is not clearly understood. Fortunately, for a CSP it is easier to provide access to content and information than to search for and implement the "killer apps" for the consumer market.

As such, the "application of applications" will focus on providing access to data, information, and content. In the consumer market, we already see this trend in video on demand from cable companies and in video podcasts that can be downloaded and played back on MP3-like devices.

The keys to these innovations are technology readiness and market maturity. Of course, technology readiness is a prerequisite. The underlying technology must be readily available and integrated with the existing infrastructure and back-end office. When the market is not ripe for certain services, customers will not subscribe to these services in large numbers, thereby eliminating the critical mass needed for a successful roll out. The challenge is to provide customer-driven services at or below market price points. This combination is essential to the success of the corporate digital ecosystem in support of the customer digital lifestyle.

It's Not That Simple

IN THE FUTURE, CONSOLIDATION will bring various partners to the table, including hardware manufacturers, software companies, and service providers. The main reason for this transformation is the change in the way computing is performed and used by consumers and enterprises (see Figure 3).

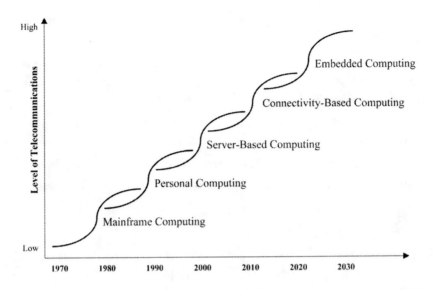

Figure 3 – Impact of Computing on Telecommunications

The increasing need for communication transcends normal Information Technology (IT)-based connectivity: Connectivity to mobile devices that users can take and use anywhere and anytime they want (also see section "The Proliferation of Edge Devices"). We are observing the first stages of this revolution in the form of the new mobile phones that incorporate music playback and download capabilities—an example of convergence of two different industries.

Impact on Communications Service Providers

TODAY'S CSPS MUST ANTICIPATE customer needs, and act quickly on those market insights. As change accelerates, CSPs must integrate, enhance and adapt offerings in a transparent manner.

The New World

BUSINESS AND CONSUMER MARKET are changing rapidly these days. It is often said that the only constant is change. Even that is no longer true in the telecom world. The rate of change is accelerating across all areas of telecom—as we have seen with the new functions and features in mobile phones.

This rate of change demands great flexibility. That is true from an enterprise perspective, as front-end and back-end systems must support the rollout of new functionality. It is also true from a consumer perspective, as consumers assimilate new technology into their day-to-day activities.

As markets mature, price pressures become inevitable. This trend requires CSPs to look for new and emerging revenue opportunities.

Maturity and Volume

WHILE ENTERPRISES TYPICALLY PURSUE the same consumer markets with similar product and service offerings, very few are sufficiently growing their market through service innovation. In an emerging market, innovation is high, but the revenue opportunity is limited (see Figure 4). As the product and associated services mature, so does the revenue stream. As the services become mainstream, innovation wanes, and as a result, so does the revenue stream. In order to maintain revenue streams, new products must be introduced, i.e. the cycle needs to start all over again.

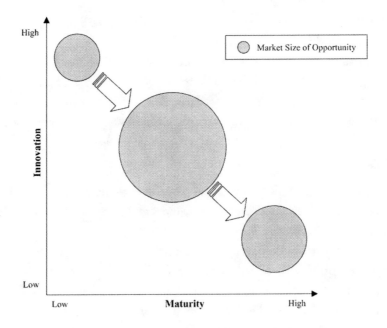

Figure 4 – Innovation and Product/Service Maturity

The ability to adopt new market and industry models will drive both innovation and demand volume. CSPs must seek a dialogue with consumers and enterprises to define what creates value for them. A CSP can also use these conversations to focus its product and service offerings and to shape demand in a market increasingly defined by extended value chains.

Convergence Meets Segmentation

THE TELECOMMUNICATIONS INDUSTRY HAS seen several cycles of convergence and divergence over the past 170 years, and the rate at which these cycles occur is accelerating.

CSPs continue to acquire customers, but overall, revenue tends to be flat due to growing competition and the accelerated rate of change. To succeed, a CSP must improve its ability to deliver unique service offerings through convergence.

At the same time, the CSP must understand its customer base and micro-segment those customers into groups that can be mapped to their service offering. Preferably, knowledge management tools should be used to identify untapped market opportunities in these micro-segmented consumer markets.

Through the combination of these two approaches (convergence and segmentation), the CSP is able to create new markets and sell more effectively to its existing consumer base. The key is creating demand and satisfying that demand instantaneously with new products and services.

New Players

WE ALL KNOW THAT "free" does not really mean free. "Free" promotions are actually to entice consumers to look and to get a feel for the underlying technologies. As soon as these technologies mature and reach the point of wide-market acceptance, large brand-oriented companies will step in and provide these services at a reasonable price and service level.

As an example, a few years ago, the free Internet telephony market had several players. This market, while still in existence, has largely been taken over by telecom and cable companies in an attempt to stop the revenue loss, and to bring new offerings to this market. These new players are attracting customers and forcing change on the original market players. The same is true for the broadband phone market.

Making It Simple

ALTHOUGH THERE IS A small market of consumers who want to be on the leading edge of technology, and are willing to pay a premium for it, most consumers are driven by speed and price. In a marketplace where major players use loyalty programs as a vehicle to accelerate the adoption of new services, price is key. Even if the price point is right, if competitors offer more speed, more minutes or more functions, consumers are willing to switch if they can get the additional functionality at little or no additional cost.

So consumers are now in the driver's seat, especially in a market where the ubiquity of the Internet makes comparison shopping extremely easy. This shift in power forces a CSP to rethink its integration and back-office interfaces. In effect, it calls for an overhaul of the complete application and infrastructure environment to make them leaner and more flexible.

Stickiness

CONSUMER STICKINESS IS ALSO important to CSPs. They must create experiences and services that appeal to consumers so that customers closely identify with those solutions. This approach to stickiness must be underpinned by a deeply entrenched knowledge management system that focuses on the consumer from a services perspective. By doing this, CSPs can create an overall experience that is personalized and memorable.

Impact on Communications Service Providers

THE TELECOM SPACE CONTINUES to change at an ever-faster pace through mergers, acquisitions and the emergence of new players. These new players carve out a niche market, attract a customer base, and start growing into areas traditionally dominated by existing CSPs. Since these new players can react quickly, an incumbent CSP must become more agile, while continuing to deliver the service and experience levels their customers expect.

The Proliferation of Edge Devices

THE PROLIFERATION OF EDGE devices is pushing demands on business to the "edge." The growing number of always-on devices—like Personal Digital Assistants (PDAs), mobile phones, toll tags and Radio Frequency Identifier (RFID) chips—is increasing the need for scale, speed and flexibility. This need can only be addressed by enabling the network to provide configuration and management to these devices in an almost automatic and automated fashion so that new functions and features can be provided seamlessly and invisibly to the consumers. This transparency is an important enabler for the emerging data-driven enterprise and consumer environments.

RFID Tags

INFORMATION HAS DRIVEN THE business world for several decades now. With the continued advance of digital technologies, both the corporate and personal environments are now ready to embrace RFIDs.

RFID devices, by enabling the remote storage and retrieval of data, will give manufacturers a far deeper understanding of consumer preferences and buying patterns. RFIDs will also have a significant impact on the consumer—as personal information is tracked and stored to make the buying experience a unique one. RFID tags can also be combined with location-based capabilities and the global presence of the CSP to deliver personalized services on-the-fly.

Machine-to-Machine

THE NETWORK IS INCREASINGLY becoming a commodity used to synchronize information. The network core stays constant, delivering high bandwidth transport that ensures an expanded market reach for each new generation of devices. This trend started with the Personal Computer (PC) and progressed through the laptop to the mobile phone and PDA.

According to several studies, the number of "things" that are going to be interconnected will soon outnumber the number of people who are connected. As pointed out before, the main reason for this proliferation is the shift of interaction from "person-to-person" to "thing-to-thing" (see Figure 1).

This change in access and usage patterns requires different support models from a telecom perspective.

Synchronization of Any Device

Consumers are now carrying several devices with them at any point in time, each of which has a dedicated function. Even though consolidation of functionality does occur, the true innovation occurs at the level of each point solution. It is the existing type of devices where additional functionality is being built in as technology matures.

This proliferation of devices calls for the need for synchronization of them. Even though a Personal Area Network (PAN) provides some synchronization function, a global capability across platforms, time zones, and network technologies is required to achieve true synchronization. Again, this type of synchronization needs to occur in a way that is transparent to the consumer.

The two trends—machine-to-machine and synchronization—imply that in essence consumers are becoming less predominant, and that machine-to-machine interactions are growing in importance.

Bluetooth

OVER THE PAST DECADE, communication has evolved from a person-to-machine-to-person protocol to a machine-to-machine protocol. With the ever-increasing pace of change, information needs to be relayed and acted upon almost instantaneously. This is especially true in the IT environment where automated changes typically require a fast, machine-enabled response, backed by access to Wide Area Networks (WANs), Metropolitan Area Networks (MANs), and Local Area Networks (LANs).

Although WAN, MAN, and LAN access remains important, short-distance machine-to-machine communication is growing in importance. The advent of a Personal Area Network (PAN)—a network that surrounds a person and the peripherals in close proximity—allows for the interaction of personal devices, regardless of the interface. This type of interaction requires the use of a common protocol that works within close proximity. Bluetooth® wireless technology is an example.

Everything Connects

IN TODAY'S SOCIETY, PEOPLE and organizations are struggling to manage information overload. The speed at which information will become available is critical to the survival of an enterprise. In fact, we could use the phrase, "Information at the speed of human thought," to depict this vision: as humans will still play a key role in the decision process, the *right information* needs to be delivered in the *right form* to the *right person* at the *right time* in the *right place* to take the *right action*[21]. This concept is referred to as the Right6.

Let's break this down into a little bit more detail:

---

[21] This concept is an extension of a concept called Right[5] introduced by EDS. EDS Corporation. EDS and Automatic Identification Using Radio Frequency Technology, October 2003.

- The *right information* is the information you need for the problem immediately at hand: this is a function of smart software agents and the concept of knowledge management.

- The *right form* is the optimal conduit for the information in the given situation. If the user is at a workstation, a Web page on displayed a PC may be the right form. But if the user is standing in front of customers, information might come in a more private way, like through a miniature earphone.

- The *right person* is a security matter. Confidential corporate information must be delivered in a secure way.

- The *right time* is just that, a matter of timing. The financial performance of an investment last year, and even last week, just isn't good enough anymore. With information changing so quickly, users want the most current information made instantly available to them.

- The *right place* is a question of mobility. By using mobile devices, users can always send, receive and store the information they want and need.

- The *right action* relates to the fact that a business function needs to be performed in line with the information provided.

These days, the right person can be a person or a "thing" or "device." More and more (decision) processes are digitized, resulting in delegated authority. This authority is delegated not only to people, but also to devices that take action on behalf of a person. A very simple example is when an online merchant, like Amazon, automatically generates a recommendation on a related product based on buying patterns of the user. As more information is made available in a digital format, digital agents will analyze that data to produce faster and more effective decisions.

The Risk Takers and the New Software ... Rules

THE OLD SAYING "NO pain, no gain" could be changed to "No change, no gain." Because in the telecommunications market change continues to accelerate due to deregulation, competition, consumer demands and technology evolution. New players are emerging that will take risks (e.g. Vonage), while outsiders are buying their way into the market (e.g., eBay acquiring Skype[22]). Similar acquisitions are taking place in the travel industry, as illustrated by the acquisition of lastminute. com by Sabre[23].

In general, these acquisitions position the acquiring company at the forefront of one or more leading technologies, allowing them to leapfrog the competition (also see Figure 4) and pursue new revenue growth.

The Value of Storing the Data

EVEN THOUGH THE NETWORK is extremely important from a corporate and personal perspective, the true value lies in the data and information traversing the network.

According to market research firm, TheInfoPro, in 2005, Storage Area Network (SAN) data will grow by 60 percent, while Network Attached Storage (NAS) data will grow at 41 percent[24]. This data will ultimately be used by consumers (either professionally or personally), thus generating additional network traffic through increased data storage and retrieval.

In the digital lifestyle, consumers want the convenience of anywhere/ anytime information. This information could be stored centrally, behind a corporate firewall, or at the end user's home. In all instances, access to the required data should be provided seamlessly, almost instantaneously, and in a secure way.

Transaction Loads

The data explosion is coming from six different sources:
1. The first is the movement to real time, or rather running in real time. It is a transition that started with mainframe batch

---

[22] skype.com. "eBay Completes Acquisition."

[23] Harteveldt, Henry H. Forrester. "Sabre/Lastminute.com — Brilliant."

[24] TheInfoPro. "Survey Says: Data growth continues its breakneck pace," December 2005.

processing and is accelerating today as companies understand the value of "now."

2. The second movement is called "Meta-bytes." It is information about information. It is the opportunity to understand the where, why, who, etc. about the information now being gathered.

3. The third represents the explosion at the edge. The embedded technology revolution has begun and is populating our world with computational devices so small as to disappear from the naked eye. Yet each of these devices has the opportunity of sending information at unprecedented levels.

4. The fourth is about the information exchange with others in the value chain. Maintaining a "four walls" restriction on customer and suppliers' information is no longer a viable option. Inter-enterprise intimacy is about understanding your customers, their customers and then their customers' information along with that of your suppliers, their suppliers and then their suppliers' information.

5. The fifth element is information that allows corporations and consumers to project current information into future possibilities: the future focus. The type, source and form of this future-oriented information vary significantly from those of traditional corporate data. This is one of the most interesting new flows of information.

6. The sixth and final element is processing speed. Even if you have the same amount of information, but you process it faster and faster, you have essentially increased the volume of information. Increased speed of business decisions, more accurate and quicker reporting of financial assets, improved visibility into operational processes all require faster and deeper information flows.

Traditional systems have a flex factor of 1, meaning that we are dealing with a "normal distribution" workload. In a Web-based environment, transactions are getting smaller and more frequent. As a result, the peak-to-average ratio will increase: a flex-factor of X. As we move toward an event-driven environment, the flex factor increases between 10 and 1,000 fold. From a CSP perspective, the latter is the type of workload that is to be expected in a consumer-driven environment with machines interacting with other machines, without human intervention.

As a result of this workload flexibility and the continued upsurge in data, transactions loads are shifting and increasing, placing additional strain on CSPs.

Anticipating Flexibility

CSPS REQUIRE SPEED TO maintain and grow market share. In order to accelerate speed-to-market, systems must be analyzed quickly, preferably in real-time, to support on-the-fly adjustments. Trend data can be used to develop, map and deliver new products and services to precisely-segmented niche markets. By fully analyzing that trend data, CSPs can better understand why consumers buy, when they are willing to churn and why they accept new content and services. In the future, the correlation of this trend data and the delivery of new services will take place in real time.

Impact on Communications Service Providers

AS NEW TECHNOLOGIES ARE introduced, CSPs must capture market share quickly. This timely reaction is important, since niche players may be able to enter the new market faster as they have little or no legacy dependence, a fact that gives them a competitive advantage. At the same time, incumbents have an advantage over new entrants, as they have an infrastructure in place that allows the scalability needed in the Internet and RFID-based world.

Device and Mode Proliferation

AS DEVICES PROLIFERATE, CONSUMERS want to take full advantage of the capabilities of the device, provided the price point is right. So the network must be able to handle the traffic flow to and from the device, not just in the customer's home market, but globally.

The Partnership of Solutions and Infrastructure

SINCE CUSTOMERS WANT TO use their devices globally, partnerships must be forged to enable solutions across geographies and infrastructures. To make these solutions economically feasible, services and marketing must be linked in a way that leverages existing infrastructures, and that drives innovation in the telecommunications and related industries.

The Business of Applications and Services

IN ORDER TO BE successful in the telecommunications space, CSPs must also offer services and application that appeal to the end user. These solutions should target specific markets, such as parents, traveling business executives, or pet or homeowners.

As an example, parents want to be sure that their children are safe when they leave the house, so providing children with a mobile phone is a natural choice. Teenagers may at times decide to ignore a phone call from home. So parents may be willing to pay for an offering that allows them (and them only) to locate the mobile phone through a built-in positioning system.

Traveling business executives may not always want to take their laptops with them. Instead they may only need a small laptop-like device (weighing only a few ounces) that can connect to the Internet to download email, calendar updates and corporate data.

Pet owners might want the ability to remotely monitor the well being of the pet. Homeowners might appreciate the ability to remotely monitor and change room temperatures, video systems or mobile device settings. The possibilities are endless.

These new packages of mobile phone, voice services and data access, bundled with content and applications, will encourage the formation of new business relationships and the emergence of new business models and markets.

The Community

THE MOBILE PHONE HAS long been a one-on-one communication vehicle. That trend is changing, as teenagers and pre-teens use phones in new and different ways: such as closely integrating instant messaging and multi-party conversations. These newer generations have taken multi-tasking to the next level on the PC and laptop and now are demanding similar capabilities on the mobile device.

It is these emerging market segments, communities and groups, that are forcing changes to services and devices. And their voices will only become more important as they enter the workforce.

Lifestyle Drivers

IN TODAY'S BUSY WORLD, consumers want to spend more time with their families and always be connected to them. As a result, the lifestyle drivers are speed, ease of use, and the availability of anywhere/anytime connectivity. The latter requirement is basically a restatement of the <u>Right</u> 6 concept.

The key applications that consumers are looking for at the moment are content related: email, phone, and calendar. The next-generation consumers are looking for rich content in the form of music, video and games.

Making the Connections

IN THE PAST, ENTERPRISES grew through acquisitions. Today, that process is too slow to allow them to expand markets quickly. As a result, virtual enterprises allow companies to join forces and respond to market opportunities in an accelerated manner. These virtual enterprises often take the form of go-to-market alliances. This approach leverages existing market knowledge to target precise market segments with specific products or services.

A number of industries are now converging to meet these new market demands. Examples include education and transportation, where converged alliances are identifying important new communications opportunities. For example, some universities are incorporating podcasts into student study materials.

By forging alliance partnerships to deliver services to the next-generation workforce (the current generation of teenagers), a CSP can position itself for growth. Astute CSPs are already seeking ways to bring converged entertainment, gaming and educational services to this emerging market segment.

The World of Utter Simplicity

THERE IS A LOT of truth in saying that a device should be so simple that a child can use it. This is especially true in the telecommunications world, where devices have an average lifetime of less than one year. This high turnover rate requires that the interface is intuitive and does not require a complex user's manual. The device interface should also be compatible with prior versions as much as possible to minimize the required learning effort.

The Commodity of Voice Transport

INTERNET PROTOCOL (IP) IS becoming the prevailing mechanism for transport of voice and data. However, data will be the key driver for most of the network traffic. Voice will become a commodity, which most likely will be bundled into offerings as a free item.

However, consumers will continue to expect enhancements in the voice area. This includes, but is not limited to: transparent global access, transparent billing and "portability-to-the-extreme." Portability is an issue because most consumers still have two phone lines: wireline and wireless. In the future, the consumers will demand that these and other types of technologies be merged into a single phone. This will allow other network technologies, such as Wireless Fidelity (WiFi), to be exploited to meet service and price expectations.

Total Transparency of Usage and the Freedom of Choice

WIRELESS AND WIRELINE CONVERGENCE is just the beginning. In the future, all types of devices will enjoy true mobility, and interconnectivity will take place at the Personal Area Network (PAN) level.

We will see devices become more powerful. They will be able to capture, restore, and push content transparently. In effect, these devices will become an extension of the owner, handling many day-to-day tasks and bothering the consumer only in the event of an exception. To enable these capabilities, CSPs must deploy networks with the bandwidth and speed needed to minimize latency while providing built-in and transparent security.

Content Is More Than King

AS MENTIONED BEFORE, CONTENT is king in the telecommunications industry. But content is more than what consumers download and consume on the spot. Over time, content may be augmented in various forms, such as an overlay to a picture taken on a mobile device that gives the consumer an "out of this world" experience.

Even though content is delivered primarily via copper at the moment, technology advances will increasingly allow content to be delivered to mobile devices. This change will allow content to be delivered in new and more cost efficient ways.

Frictionless

TODAY'S CONSUMERS DON'T CARE where information comes from or how it is delivered. They just want to use and enjoy that information. To meet those expectations, the telecommunications industry must shift its focus away from technology and toward consumer-oriented solutions, and look for a more collaborative market model. This future vision will require more closely integrated systems, an objective that can be reached in a timely manner only through the use of open Application Programming Interfaces (APIs), based on industry-accepted standards.

Full Coverage

AS SOON AS OPEN APIs exist and are implemented globally, true interoperability and seamless integration can occur. This integration will result in full coverage for both voice and data (to the point that native language support will be provided anywhere in the world, as devices "know" their consumers and their preferences).

By linking any device through any network seamlessly wherever and whenever the device is used, customers strengthen their grip on the consumer-driven economy. Thus more choices will become available globally at the touch of a keyboard, or preferably, at the request of a voice command.

Self Provisioning

CONSEQUENTLY, CONSUMERS WILL FEEL increasingly empowered to make decisions themselves using information that is readily available through the ubiquitous Internet. The next logical step is for consumers to expect and demand self-provisioning capabilities. To meet the coming demand for self-service and self-provisioning, CSPs must assemble optimized, consumer-oriented demand chains—and move from a corporation-driven supply chain to a consumer-driven demand chain.

Impact on Communications Service Providers

END USERS WILL BE and should be the center of this emerging CSP marketplace. As consumers become more tech-savvy, the speed, rate, and timing of new service roll outs will no longer be driven purely by the CSPs. Instead, end users will have a greater influence on the services provided and products supported by the CSPs. To meet the needs of these increasingly agile consumers, CSPs must become truly agile providers.

Conclusion

IN TODAY'S FAST CHANGING environment, yesterday's world of vendor- and product-driven marketing has been replaced by consumer- and service-driven demand. As a result of this shift, the focus of the telecommunications industry is that of a telecommunications-driven digital ecosystem in support of the consumer-driven digital lifestyle.

In this competitive environment, the CSP not only needs to be aware of customer demands and wishes, but also it needs to respond quickly to changing market signals. These changes cascade from customer requirements to provisioning, content and eventually to the underlying IT infrastructure—an infrastructure that must evolve to adapt to changing market conditions.

Those CSPs that adapt to this new world will reap the benefits of increased customer loyalty and market share. A CSP that accomplishes this will become a market leader that can shape the market and drive it to new heights.

About the Author

René J. Aerdts, Ph.D., is an EDS fellow. He is part of the Information Technology Outsourcing (ITO) Service Delivery organization, which is responsible for the IT component service delivery. The title of EDS fellow is awarded to the corporation's most innovative thought leaders in recognition of their exceptional achievements. As an EDS fellow, Aerdts helps to develop enterprise-wide initiatives that shape the future of EDS. He leads the EDS Fellows Program activities for clients in the communications industry.

Conclusion and Outlook

René J. Aerdts, Ph.D.
Andreas G. Bauer
Max R. Speur

Why We Wrote This Book

WE HAD ONE MAJOR goal in mind when we created this book. We wanted to present our consolidated views on how you, as a Communications Service Provider (CSP), can reshape your business to achieve three fundamental goals:

- Systematic cost containment
- Superior customer experience
- Sustainable revenue growth and customer loyalty

The book evolves around two overarching themes: how the CSP can transform toward a future state and how the CSP can balance the three goals mentioned above.

What We Hope We Have Achieved

THIS BOOK IS A true representation of EDS' desire to be an insightful resource that provides leading-edge thinking and innovation. We believe the methods and processes described in this book will help your enterprise increase speed to market and optimize business value.

The contributors of this book are leading industry experts, who in their professional lives, have faced situations similar to those described in this book. We used that experience to build a book that we hope serves as a tool or guide for you when your company faces transformation challenges.

How We Hope You Will Use This Book

THIS BOOK BRINGS TOGETHER thought leadership and discusses compelling reasons for change. It provides recommended approaches on how to manage that change successfully. We hope it provides answers to solving issues that are important to you. We hope that you will embrace the concepts we described and contact us so that we can discuss how to embark on a transformational journey together. We invite you to go to eds.com to learn more about EDS.

What Is the Future Going To Look Like?

WE WANT TO SHARE our thoughts with you about the future. It is our belief that the next-generation CSP needs to focus its attention on those aspects of the business that provide the most value, requiring the CSP to shift its focus from infrastructure and technology-based products to next-generation services to create customer intimacy. First, and foremost, these services are the distinguishing factors that contribute to the customer's experience. Secondly, as these services generate sustainable revenue streams, they are key for a CSP to recoup investments in network and IT infrastructures.

However, in order to determine the long-term future of the CSP, we need to analyze market and industry trends, both from a technology and business perspective. Figure 1 depicts nine future trends.

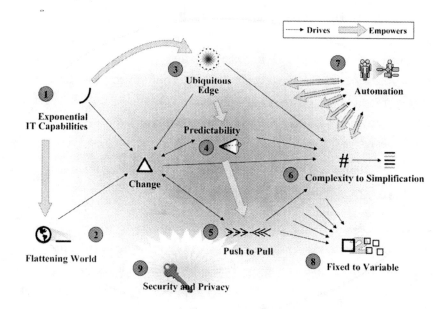

Figure 1 – Nine Future Trends

All the elements in Figure 1 are built on the notion of continuous change. Although this view provides a safe bet, it is critical to note that the view on the future is being challenged on a regular basis, and adjustments are being made as appropriate.

In Table 1, we provide our vision on these nine trends and their impact on CSPs. You can see that the topics in this book address many of these trends. We hope you find our views relevant and valuable for your business.

#	Trend	Driver	Challenge	Call for Action
1	Exponential Information Technology (IT) Capabilities	The continued rapid advances in IT capabilities and decreases in costs will drive accelerating change.	How can CSPs discover new ways to exploit these capabilities for competitive advantage in the ICT marketplace?	• Build an ecosystem of partners to drive revenue growth in the ICT market. • Build a service delivery environment to support converged ICT services in an end-to-end fashion. • Use improved IT capabilities to simulate business decisions before they are released.
2	Flattening World	The "flat world" will amplify the effects of the leveled playing field by creating new markets as well as competitors and uneven economics.	How can a CSP take advantage of a global workforce, exploit new emerging markets and protect its customer and revenue base against market entry of global players?	• Deploy global processes and virtual infrastructures to operate front-office, back-office and enterprise management processes in an insistent way, taking advantage of the globalization of the workforce for contact and shared services centers. • Create an agile application architecture that allows easy incorporation of new businesses while assuring global consistency. • Acknowledge the probability of having new competition as well as new customers. • Build an ecosystem of best-of-class partners on a global basis. • Develop the ability to accelerate time-to-market while building on an existing knowledge base on customers and local markets.

Table 1 – Drivers and Impact of the Nine Future Trends

#	Trend	Driver	Challenge	Call for Action
3	Ubiquitous Edge	The "edge" (first contact of the user with an application) will continue to expand and disappear into the environment, creating an exponential growth of context information.	How can the proliferation and convergence of devices be turned into new business opportunities and ways to create a superior end-user experience?	• Simplify the service offerings and evolve them into easy-to-use quadruple plays in order to "own the home." • Create and offer enterprise-grade applications to enable businesses to take full advantage of new devices. • Offer world-class customer support around an ever-increasing range of end user devices. • Understand and exploit the positioning of CSPs in obtaining and distributing contextual edge information.
4	Predictability	The speed of change and reduced time for response will drive companies from a reactive "sense and respond" to a proactive "cause and effect" positioning.	How can CSPs detect patterns of the wants and needs of customers in the ever-lasting search for the "killer" application?	• Gauge early-adopter demand by rapidly introducing emerging products, and converting them into mainstream product offerings. • Create the ability to launch services rapidly and retire them based on an agile service creation environment, partner programs and rigorous service management.

Table 1 – Drivers and Impact of the Nine Future Trends *continued*

#	Trend	Driver	Challenge	Call for Action
5	**Push to Pull**	Consumers and customers will demand personalized interactions that tailor both "bits and atoms" to their individual wants and needs.	How can CSPs focus on demand-side economics by gauging customers' wants and needs to create superior services and customer experiences to match them?	• Reverse the old paradigm "We build it; they will come" by proactively monitoring consumer trends and analyze business value chains, to be able to create services that add true value to the customer. • Create a single view of the customer. • Tune applications to be customer and service centric rather than CSP centric. • Learn from innovative new business models in order to create new services or maximize existing revenue streams.
6	**Complexity to Simplification**	The proliferation of change and new capabilities will create a more complex world that will exceed the hrair[25] of companies and consumers.	How can CSPs create simplified user interfaces and service offerings and provide an easy way of doing business with them?	• Create a seamless entry door to the CSP across all customer touch points and along all "moments of truth." • Create a seamless customer experience across all network technologies to achieve true convergence. • Create simple user interfaces that allow end users to buy, activate, personalize and use new services with a few clicks.

Table 1 – Drivers and Impact of the Nine Future Trends *continued*

---

[25] In this case, <u>hrair</u> (defined as the coincidences between the channel capacity of a number of human cognitive and perceptual tasks) refers to the capability of companies and consumers to absorb and incorporate new products or services, without eliminating an existing one.

#	Trend	Driver	Challenge	Call for Action
7	Automation	The speed of business will transcend the ability of humans to manage and operate it directly.	How can CSPs leverage a new level of automation to streamline business processes and facilitate activation and use of new services.	• Optimize front-office/back-office integration through flow through processing. • Automate provisioning processes for both, communications and IT services and maximize the use of self-service mechanisms. • Automate service delivery and assurance to allow true end-to-end management of quality of service.
8	**Fixed to Variable**	Rapid change and new business models will require flexibility and variability in the procurement and management of all resources.	How can a CSP leverage capabilities, skills and resources within its ecosystem of partners to be able to focus on providing superior service?	• Create ecosystems of partners to be able to leverage their existing capabilities and optimize asset utilization. • Create virtual environments for computing, contact and shared services center to optimize load balancing. • Provide scalable and leveraged environments for service delivery. • Move closer to a variablized workforce.

Table 1 – Drivers and Impact of the Nine Future Trends *continued*

#	Trend	Driver	Challenge	Call for Action
9	Security and Privacy	Security will be enabled by a logic-based, multi-tiered environment that is context respectful in enabling access while deterring malware. Privacy must be controlled by individuals.	How can CSPs create an environment with built-in (rather than bolted-on) security that is a multi-layer, context aware managed asset? How can the cultural shift of giving privacy control to customers be adequately managed?	• Understand future threats to security and proactively take steps to eliminate them. • Drive security to the application logic layer, not just at the perimeter. • Embrace the concept that customers "own" the CSP's content and enable them with active control.

Table 1 – Drivers and Impact of the Nine Future Trends *continued*

About the Authors

René J. Aerdts, Ph.D., is an EDS fellow. He is part of the Information Technology Outsourcing (ITO) Service Delivery organization, which is responsible for the IT component service delivery. The title of EDS fellow is awarded to the corporation's most innovative thought leaders in recognition of their exceptional achievements. As an EDS fellow, Aerdts helps to develop enterprise-wide initiatives that shape the future of EDS. He leads the EDS Fellows Program activities for clients in the communications industry.

Andreas G. Bauer is the global leader of Communications Industry Frameworks in EDS Portfolio Development. He has over 18 years of experience in business consulting and technology enablement, including careers with IBM Global Services, Deloitte Consulting and Dr. Göhring & Partner Management Consultants. He specializes in marketing and

IT strategies, process design and reengineering, IT planning, and management of system implementation projects.

Max R. Speur has had significant international experience in the communications industry in Europe and Asia Pacific. He is currently the Asia Pacific communications industry leader for EDS. In this role, Speur is responsible for innovation, thought leadership and demand creation, and for enabling clients' growth. Speur was with IBM Global Services previously, where he served as business development executive on a variety of engagements in Thailand, China, India and Australia.

Terminology

AAA – Authentication, Authorization and Accounting
API – Application Programming Interface
ARPU – Average Revenue per User
BA – Business Architecture
BATOG – Business Context, Application Portfolio, Technology
 Infrastructure, Organizational Capability, Governance
BI – Business Intelligence
BSS – Business Support System
CAGR – Compound Annual Growth Rate
Capex – Capital expenditure
CC&B – Customer Care and Billing
CDP – Continuous Data Protection
COTS – Commercial Off-the-Shelf Software
CRM – Customer Relationship Management
CSP – Communications Service Provider
CSR – Customer Service Representative
CTI – Computer/Telephony Integration
DSL – Digital Subscriber Line
DVD – Digital Versatile Disc
EBITDA – Earnings Before Interest, Tax, Depreciation and
 Amortization
eBPP – electronic Bill Presentment and Payment
EDA – Event-Driven Architecture
ERP – Enterprise Resource Planning
eTOM – enhanced Telecom Operations Map®
F&A – Finance and Administration

FCAPS – Fault, Configuration, Accounting, Performance and
 Security
FTE – Full-Time Equivalent
FTTC – Fiber To The Curb
FTTP – Fiber To The Premises
HR – Human Resources
ICE – Information, Communication and Entertainment
ICT – Information and Communications Technology
ILM – Information Lifecycle Management
IM – Instant Messaging
IMS – IP Multimedia Subsystem
IN – Intelligent Network
IPS – Integrated Process Model
IP – Internet Protocol
IPTV – Internet Protocol Television
ISO – International Organization for Standardization
ISV – Independent Software Vendor
IS – Information Services
IT – Information Technology
ITO – Information Technology Outsourcing
ITIL – Information Technology Infrastructure Library
IVR – Interactive Voice Response
KPI – Key Performance Indicator
LAN – Local Area Network
MAN – Metropolitan Area Network
MSO – Multiple Service Operator
NAS – Network Attached Storage
NGN – Next Generation Network
Netco – Network Company
NGOSS – New-Generation Operations Systems and Software
Opex – Operating Expenditure
Opco – Operations Company
OSS – Operations Support System
OSS/BSS – Operations Support System/Business Support System
P&L – Profit & Loss

PAN – Personal Area Network
PC – Personal Computer
PDA – Personal Digital Assistant
PIM– Personal Information Management
PLM – Product Lifecycle Management
PSTN – Public Switched Telephone Network
QoS – Quality of Service
RFID – Radio Frequency Identifier
SAN – Storage Area Network
SCE – Service Creation Environment
SDK – Software Development Kit
SDP – Service Delivery Platform
Servco – Service Company
SDP – Service Delivery Platform
SI – Systems Integrator
SID – Shared Information/Data Model
SIP – Session Initiated Protocol
SLA – Service Level Agreement
SMP – Service Management Platform
SOA – Service Oriented Architecture
SOHO – Small Office/Home Office
SME – Small and Medium Enterprise
SSC – Shared Services Center
STB – Set Top Box
TMF – TeleManagement Forum
TAM – Telecom Applications Map
TNA – Technology Neutral Architecture
VAR – Value Added Reseller
VOD – Video On Demand
VoIP – Voice over Internet Protocol
WAN – Wide Area Network
WiFi – Wireless Fidelity
WiMAX – Worldwide Interoperability for Microwave Access
WLAN – Wireless Local Area Network
XML – Extensible Markup Language

About the Contributors

Lead Team

René J. Aerdts, Ph.D., is an EDS fellow. He is part of the Information Technology Outsourcing (ITO) Service Delivery organization, which is responsible for the IT component service delivery. The title of EDS fellow is awarded to the corporation's most innovative thought leaders in recognition of their exceptional achievements. As an EDS fellow, Aerdts helps to develop enterprise-wide initiatives that shape the future of EDS. He leads the EDS Fellows Program activities for clients in the communications industry.

Andreas G. Bauer is the global leader of Communications Industry Frameworks in EDS Portfolio Development. He has over 18 years of experience in business consulting and technology enablement, including careers with IBM Global Services, Deloitte Consulting and Dr. Göhring & Partner Management Consultants. He specializes in marketing and IT strategies, process design and reengineering, IT planning, and management of system implementation projects.

Max R. Speur has had significant international experience in the communications industry in Europe and Asia Pacific. He is currently the Asia-Pacific communications industry leader for EDS. In this role, Speur is responsible for innovation, thought leadership and demand creation, and for enabling clients' growth. Speur was with IBM Global Services previously, where he served as business development executive on a variety of engagements in Thailand, China, India and Australia.

Contributors

Alberto Balestrazzi is a client industry executive at EDS for major telecom accounts in Europe, Middle East and Africa (EMEA). He is responsible for innovation, thought leadership and demand creation, and for enabling growth and transformation for clients. He brings more than 18 years of experience in the communications industry. He has worked as a management and technology consultant for major operators across Europe. Balestrazzi has held leadership roles with IBM, A.T. Kearney, Booz Allen Hamilton and Accenture.

Sebastião M. Burin is a client executive for the Communications Industry in EDS Latin America. He is responsible for building and sustaining strong relationships with clients and for developing new business opportunities for EDS. Burin's experience spans over 20 years in the IT industry, including a career with Booz Allen Hamilton. He has significant experience in systems development and consulting for a variety of industries, especially telecommunications and financial services. Burin specializes in IT strategy and IT transformation, from definition through implementation.

Sue Chevins leads the EDS Global Communications Industry organization. She has an extensive background in business and technology consulting in the telecommunications industry—both on the sales and delivery side of the industry. Chevins has over 20 years of experience in various leadership positions. Chevins was a vice president at Capgemini and global sales officer for its North American organization. She also served as chief people officer for the merger of Capgemini and Ernst & Young for the Telecom, Media and Entertainment business unit.

Jürgen Donnerstag is a chief architect with the EDS Europe, Middle East and Africa (EMEA) Communications Industry organization and member of the EMEA Architects' Office. He is responsible for providing consistent architecture guidance and support to communication projects and proposals across Europe. He has more than 14 years of experience in developing applications, integration and enterprise architectures. His current area of special interest is service oriented architectures for the communications industry.

Vinod Krishnan is an enterprise architect at EDS with over 10 years of experience in the Communications Industry. He specializes in developing IT strategies and architectures, defining systems integration solutions and creating IT transformation road maps to enable clients to respond to business imperatives. Vinod is currently working on solutions for next-generation data and IPTV services.

Paul M. Morrison is a client industry executive in the EDS Global Communications Industry Group. He has more than 20 years of experience in management and information technology, supporting telecommunications clients in the Americas, Europe, Middle East, Africa and Asia that are in the midst of significant change. Previously, he was a partner and executive at IBM Global Services and also had careers at A.T. Kearney, McKinsey and BP.

Renato Osato is a client industry executive for the Communications Industry in Latin America. He is responsible for innovation, thought leadership, demand creation, and for enabling growth and transformation for clients. He has over 17 years of professional experience in IT, with previous careers at Unisys, Telemar and Accenture. He served a number of communications clients around Latin America, including fixed-line carriers, cellular companies and pay-TV operators. Osato specializes in IT planning and systems integration implementation.

Timothy C. Samler is a member of the Communications Industry Frameworks team in EDS Portfolio Development. He has over 20 years experience in the communications industry in sales, marketing and IT management, including careers with KPMG Management Consulting, Oracle, Nortel Networks and Telus Canada. He is the co-author of the book *Delighting Customers: How to Win and Retain Loyal Customers*.

Harvey R.A. Stotland is a client industry executive with the EDS Global Communications Industry group. He has over 16 years of experience in management and IT consulting, systems integration and outsourcing, including careers with IBM, A.T. Kearney and Hewlett-Packard. He specializes in business performance improvement, product strategy and implementation, IT strategy, architecture and planning and in the management of IT-based business transformation programs.

Tara L. Whitehead is a client industry executive with the EDS Global Communications Industry group. She has over 16 years of experience in the telecommunications industry and IT consulting, including careers with the Department of Commerce's U.S. & Foreign Commercial Service Division in the Netherlands; IBM Corporation; and IBM Global Services, for Europe, Middle East and Africa. She has spearheaded the IPTV internal taskforce to define the EDS proposition. She also helps clients build capabilities to deliver next-generation services and customer care support. She specializes in next-generation solutions and IT transformation projects.

Printed in the United States
65491LVS00003B/190-384